Neuro Linguistic Pro

A User Manual For Your Brain

NLP FOR Health & Happiness

"Unlocking Your Full Potential for Well-Being and Joy"

ABHA BHARDWAJ SHARMA

Information

© 2024 by Abha Bhardwaj Sharma. All rights reserved. No part of this publication may be reproduced, distributed, or transmitted in any form or by any means, including photocopying, recording, or other electronic or mechanical methods, without the prior written permission of the publisher, except in the case of brief quotations embodied in critical reviews and certain other noncommercial uses permitted by copyright law.

The exercises, techniques, and insights presented in this book are based on the author's own experiences, learnings, and interpretation of information available in the public domain. While they have been carefully curated to assist readers in personal transformation and financial empowerment, individual results may vary.

Readers are encouraged to approach the content with an open mind and to adapt the techniques as they see fit for their personal growth and development.

Preface

The human mind, a labyrinth of neurons and synapses, shapes our thoughts, emotions, and well-being. Within this maze lies vast potential for health, happiness, and harmony, though accessing it remains elusive to many. Enter Neuro-Linguistic Programming (NLP) - a discipline combining neuroscience, psychology, and linguistics, designed to navigate the mind's intricacies and unlock holistic wellness.

This book presents a deep dive into NLP, illuminating its core principles and practical techniques. As you journey through its pages, you'll explore powerful tools such as visualisation, positive language, anchoring, and belief-change methods. With relatable anecdotes and straightforward instructions, these once-esoteric concepts will become accessible tools for daily life.

But this isn't just an instruction manual; it's a call to action. While the book equips you with knowledge, genuine transformation arises from your intent, practice, and dedication. Remember, the quest for self-improvement is ongoing, with NLP as your guide.

As you immerse yourself in this exploration, approach with openness and curiosity. This book aims to catalyse a transformation, aligning you with your aspirations and a life of holistic well-being.
Embark on this NLP journey, unlocking a refined, reenergised version of yourself.

Let the discovery begin.

A Trilogy

"Unlocking Your Brain's Potential: A User Manual"

Part 1: NLP for Health & Happiness

In the fast-paced modern world, understanding and harnessing the power of your brain is essential for leading a fulfilling life. Welcome to Part 1 of our series, **"NLP for Health & Happiness."** This installment explores how Neuro-Linguistic Programming (NLP) can be your guide to cultivating optimal well-being and a joyful existence. Through the lens of NLP, we'll delve into techniques that help you rewire your thoughts, communicate effectively, and navigate challenges, all while fostering a lasting sense of happiness and vitality.

Part 2: NLP for Wealth

Embark on a journey to unlock the potential of your brain in the realm of wealth and abundance. **In Part 2 of our series, "NLP for Wealth,"** we explore the fascinating ways NLP can reshape your financial mindset, enhance your decision-making skills, and open doors to opportunities. Discover how your thoughts, beliefs, and language play a pivotal role in attracting prosperity. Whether you're seeking financial freedom, professional success, or a secure future, this part of the series equips you with the tools to manifest wealth with intention and clarity.

Part 3: NLP for Love, Romance & Relationships

Love is a cornerstone of human existence, and your brain plays a central role in shaping the dynamics of your relationships. In Part 3 of our series, **"NLP for Love, Romance & Relationships,"** we delve into the intricacies of human connections. Explore how NLP techniques can enrich your communication, deepen your understanding of emotions, and pave the way for harmonious relationships. Whether you're seeking lasting love, enriching your partnerships, or enhancing your social interactions, this part of the series empowers you to create meaningful and fulfilling bonds.

Join us on this transformative journey as we unlock the intricacies of your brain's potential. From health and happiness to wealth and relationships, NLP becomes your compass, guiding you towards a life of enriched experiences, personal growth, and boundless possibilities.

HEALTH & HAPPINESS

A Guide to Cultivating Well-Being and Joy,"

In our fast-paced world, the pursuit of health and happiness takes centre stage as an essential endeavor. This book, **"Health & Happiness: A Guide to Cultivating Well-Being and Joy,"** serves as your comprehensive companion on the journey to creating a life of balance and fulfillment.

In the fabric of our lives, the threads of physical wellness and emotional contentment are intricately woven. We all share the aspiration to lead lives that are both healthy and brimming with happiness. Yet, amid the plethora of information, trends, and advice, it's often challenging to navigate the route that leads us to our desired destination.

Within these pages, we embark on an exploration that uncovers the intricate interplay between health and happiness. We delve deep into the mosaic of well-being, uncovering how vitality of body aligns harmoniously with tranquility of mind and heart. From the choices we make about nourishment and physical activity to the attitude we nurture and the connections we foster, every facet of existence contributes to shaping our holistic well-being.

This book is thoughtfully divided into chapters that illuminate vital facets of health and happiness. We unravel the science behind physical well-being, delve into the power of a positive outlook, offer practical strategies for managing stress, delve into nurturing relationships, and uncover the art of infusing life with purpose and significance.
As we journey together, you'll discover evidence-backed insights, actionable suggestions, and pragmatic steps that empower you to

steer your health and happiness toward the path you envision. We'll also explore innovative approaches, such as Neuro-Linguistic Programming (NLP), which can enable you to rewire your thoughts and behaviors, enhancing your ability to cultivate a life of fulfillment.

Remember, your odyssey towards health and happiness is uniquely yours. This book stands as your compass, adaptable to your circumstances, and open to your interpretation. For the pursuit of well-being and joy is not a static destination, but an ongoing expedition. May this book ignite inspiration within you and empower you to traverse this journey with intention, resilience, and a profound dedication to your holistic welfare.
Wishing you an enriching and jubilant journey ahead,

SECTION A

HEALTH

"Optimal Well-Being: Nurturing Health through NLP"

CONTENTS

SECTION A: HEALTH "Optimal Well-Being: Nurturing Health through NLP"
INTRODUCTION
Chapter 1: Brain Neurons & Neuroplasticity
Chapter 2: Neuroplasticity Negative & Positive Inputs
Chapter 3: Neural rewiring through NLP
Chapter 4: Anchoring
Chapter 5: Positive Language
Chapter 6: Visualisation
Chapter 7: Positive Affirmation
Chapter 8: Deep breathing
Chapter 9: Self Hypnosis
Chapter 10: Submodalities
Chapter 11: Belief Change
Chapter 12 The Meta-Model and Milton Model

Section B: HAPPINESS "Harmonising Life's Pleasures"

1. How to be Happy
2. Unhappiness
3. Vices:The cause of Our Unhappiness
4. Emotional Toll
5. Jealousy

6. People's Opinion
7. Learn How not to Care
8. Building Confidence
9. Self Worth
10. Contentment & Fulfilment
11. Inner Satisfaction
12. Say No to Competition
13. Compassion
14. Awareness
15. Positive Neural Pathways
16. Exercise
17. Happy Hormones
18. Stress Hormones
19. Pet & Happy Hormones
20. Emotional Health & Happiness
21. Empathy
22. Indifference
23. Excessive Engagement
24. Pursuit to Happiness
25. Higher Quality of Life
26. Shifting Perspective
27. Relationships
28. The Truth
29. Rewiring
30. DREAM, ASK, BELIEVE, RECEIVE, REPEAT "The Cycle of Manifestation"
31. Brain-training

INTRODUCTION

Life is the incredible journey of living. It's everything you experience from the day you're born to the day you pass away. It's made up of all the things you do, the people you meet, and the moments you have. Imagine life as a big puzzle – every day, you're adding new pieces to it. Some pieces are happy, like when you laugh with friends or achieve something you're proud of. Other pieces might be a bit tough, like when things don't go as planned or you feel sad.

Life is about learning and growing, just like how you learn new things at school. It's also about being with your family and friends, and making memories together. Sometimes, life can surprise you with exciting adventures or challenges that help you become stronger. And just like how you have dreams for the future, life is also about chasing your dreams and making them come true.

Think of life as a big adventure you're on. Every day, you experience different things – some good, some not-so-good. Happiness is like a treasure you find on this adventure. It's that warm, fuzzy feeling you get when something makes you smile or feel good inside.

When you have fun with your friends, enjoy your favorite meal, or achieve something you've been working on, that's life giving you happy moments. And when you feel happy, it's like a spark that lights up your adventure. It makes the journey more exciting and helps you keep going even when things get tough.

When you're happy – like when you're laughing, playing, or doing things you enjoy – it's like giving your body a little boost. Happy feelings can help your body stay strong and work well.

When you're happy, your brain releases special chemicals that can make you feel good. And when you feel good, it's like your body gets a nice message that everything is okay. This can help your immune system, which is like your body's superhero that fights off germs.

Plus, when you're happy, you might want to do things that are good for your body, like eating yummy and healthy foods or going for a walk. So, happiness isn't just about feeling great in your heart – it's also a way to help your body stay healthy and strong!

Health is how well your body and mind work together to help you feel good and do things you like. There are two main types of health: physical and mental.

Physical health is about your body working well. It means you have energy, you can run and play, and you don't feel sick all the time. Eating good food, moving your body with exercise, and sleeping enough help keep your body healthy.

Mental health is about how you feel inside your mind. It's feeling happy, not too worried, and being able to think clearly. Talking to friends, doing things you enjoy, and taking breaks when you're stressed help your mind stay healthy.

Ideal health means both your body and mind are in great shape. It's when you have lots of energy, can think clearly, and feel happy most of the time. To have ideal health, it's important to eat well, exercise, rest, and take care of your feelings.

Remember, everyone's ideal health might be a bit different, so it's about finding what makes you feel your best in both your body and your mind.

BUT….Life isn't always smooth sailing, and there are various factors that can get in the way of our health and happiness. These challenges are like hurdles that can sometimes make it hard to achieve our ideal life. Stress, which comes from everyday worries and pressures, can weigh us down and affect both our mood and our physical well-being.

Unhealthy habits like not eating well, skipping exercise, and not getting enough sleep can drain our energy and impact our physical health. Illnesses can strike unexpectedly, leaving us feeling unwell and disrupting our sense of well-being. Negative relationships or interactions with people who don't treat us kindly can take a toll on our mental health.

Financial problems, like worrying about money or not having enough resources, can add stress and anxiety to our lives. Loss, whether it's losing a loved one or facing other types of losses, can bring sadness and shake our sense of happiness. When things don't go as planned or we face disappointment, it can affect our mood and outlook on life. Environmental factors such as pollution or unsafe living conditions can impact both our health and our overall contentment. Feeling isolated or disconnected from others can lead to feelings of loneliness and unhappiness. Negative thinking patterns and low self-esteem can take a toll on our mental well-being. Past trauma or difficult experiences can cast a shadow on our overall happiness.

Despite these challenges, it's important to remember that resilience and coping strategies can help us navigate these hurdles. Seeking support from friends, family, or professionals, practicing self-care, and focusing on the positive aspects of life can contribute to better health and increased happiness, even in the face of difficulties.

The challenges that we face in life can have a significant impact on both our physical and mental health. When we encounter stressors such as work pressure, personal problems, or difficult situations, our bodies can react with physical symptoms like headaches, muscle tension, and upset stomachs.

Chronic stress, which often stems from these challenges, can weaken our immune systems, making us more vulnerable to illnesses and chronic health conditions like heart disease and diabetes. Additionally, an unhealthy lifestyle that includes poor nutrition, lack of exercise, and insufficient sleep can lead to weight gain, reduced energy levels, and increased risk of chronic diseases.

On the mental health front, challenges can give rise to negative emotions such as anxiety, sadness, and frustration. These emotions, if left unmanaged, can contribute to mental health issues like depression. Negative experiences can also erode our self-esteem and self-confidence, making it harder to navigate life's challenges.

Social isolation due to strained relationships or lack of support can lead to feelings of loneliness, which can exacerbate mental health problems. Furthermore, facing trauma or challenging events can trigger conditions like post-traumatic stress disorder (PTSD), impacting our ability to cope and manage daily life.

It's important to recognize that the connection between physical and mental health is intricate and bidirectional. Poor physical health can contribute to mental health struggles, and untreated mental health concerns can manifest as physical symptoms. To ensure overall well-being, it's crucial to address challenges in a comprehensive manner, seeking help from healthcare professionals, therapists, and support networks. By taking care of both our physical and mental health, we can better navigate life's obstacles and work toward a healthier and happier life.

It's like this: sometimes when we're stressed out in our mind – feeling worried or upset – it can end up affecting our body too. This doesn't mean all diseases come only from stress, but stress can play a part in making some health issues worse.

When we're super stressed, our body can react in ways that aren't so good for us. It might make us feel tired, give us headaches, or even mess with our stomach. Stress can also make it harder for our body to fight off sickness.our brain has a big say in our physical and mental health. Think of it like the boss of our body – it controls lots of important things. When we feel happy, scared, or even when we're hungry, it's because of our brain sending signals. The brain helps manage stuff like how fast our heart beats, how we breathe, and even how our body fights off germs. When we're stressed, the brain releases special chemicals that can affect how our body works and even how we feel inside.
Our brain also handles our feelings. When we're happy or sad, different parts of the brain are at work. It's like having an emotion control center in our head.
And here's something cool: the brain and body talk to each other. The brain listens to what's happening in our body, like if we're in pain or if we're tired. And the body also listens to the brain – if we think something will help us feel better, sometimes it actually does!
Our brain is like a super boss that keeps an eye on both our body and our mind, making sure everything is working as it should.

Chapter1: Brain, Neurons & Neuroplasticity

Brain Neurons & Neuroplasticity

The brain is composed of billions of neurons, each functioning like a tiny electrical switch. These neurons communicate with each other through electrical impulses and chemical signals, forming intricate networks that process information, control movements, regulate emotions, and more.

Neuroplasticity, often referred to as "brain plasticity," is the brain's incredible ability to change and adapt throughout our lives. It's like the brain's way of rewiring itself in response to experiences, learning, and environmental changes. This phenomenon challenges the traditional notion that the brain's structure is fixed and unchangeable after a certain age.

Types of Neuroplasticity:
Structural Plasticity: This involves physical changes in the brain's structure. Neurons can form new connections (synapses) or strengthen existing ones. They can also change their shape and form new pathways in response to learning or injury.

Functional Plasticity: This refers to the brain's ability to reorganize its functions. If one area of the brain is damaged, other areas can sometimes take over its functions. For example, after an injury, other parts of the brain might learn to control movements or sensations.

How Neuroplasticity Works:
When we learn new things, our brain forms new connections between neurons. This is like building new bridges between cities. The more we practice and learn, the stronger these connections become. If we stop using a certain skill or memory, the brain may weaken those connections to free up space for other things.
Neuroplasticity in Action:

Learning and Memory: When we learn something new, like playing an instrument or speaking a new language, our brain physically changes. Neurons involved in that skill form stronger connections, making it easier for us to remember and perform.

Recovery from Injury: After brain injury, other parts of the brain can sometimes take over the functions of damaged areas. This rewiring helps people regain lost functions through rehabilitation and practice.

Adapting to Changes: As we age, the brain can adapt to changes, helping us maintain cognitive function. It's like the brain's way of staying flexible and resilient.

Harnessing Neuroplasticity:
We can intentionally harness neuroplasticity by engaging in activities that challenge our brain, such as learning new skills, reading, puzzles, or playing musical instruments. Regular physical exercise, a healthy diet, and adequate sleep also support neuroplasticity.

In essence, the dynamic interaction between neurons and the brain's remarkable ability to adapt through neuroplasticity underpins our capacity to learn, grow, recover from challenges, and continuously shape our cognitive and emotional experiences.
Our neurons play a vital role in how the mind and body respond to stress. When we're stressed, our brain and neurons are in action to help us cope with the situation

Stress Response: When your brain senses stress, it activates the body's "fight or flight" response. Neurons release chemicals that trigger a chain reaction, preparing your body to deal with the stressor. This might make your heart beat faster, your muscles tense, and your senses more alert.

Neurons and Hormones: Neurons in your brain communicate with other parts of your body through chemicals called hormones. During stress, hormones like adrenaline and cortisol are released. These hormones prepare your body to handle challenges, boost your energy, and focus your attention.

Calming Down: After the stress is over, other neurons help calm your body down. They release chemicals that relax your muscles, slow your heart rate, and bring your body back to a more balanced state.

Adaptation: Neurons also help your brain adapt to stress over time. When you face stress repeatedly, your brain learns to handle it better. This is like practicing a sport – the more you practice, the better you become.

Coping Strategies: Neurons help you develop coping strategies to deal with stress. Activities like deep breathing, meditation, or talking to someone can activate neurons that help calm your mind and reduce stress.

Memory and Learning: Neurons play a role in how we remember and learn from stressful experiences. These experiences can teach our brain how to respond in the future and help us better manage stress.

So, yes, your neurons are like helpers that work together with your brain and body to manage stress. They enable your body to respond, adapt, and find ways to cope with different situations, helping you stay balanced and healthy.

The brain and neurons work together to adapt and respond to different situations, is indeed a part of neuroplasticity. Neuroplasticity is the brain's ability to change and reorganize itself based on experiences, learning, and even dealing with stress.

When you face stress, your brain and neurons can change their connections and responses to help you manage and cope better in the future. It's like your brain's way of learning from challenges and becoming more resilient. So, the process of your neurons helping you handle stress is a great example of how neuroplasticity works!

If neurons are consistently exposed to negative inputs like negative thoughts, challenging environments, difficult relationships, failures, and financial stress, it can have a significant impact on your mental and emotional well-being.
Let's break down how this can affect you:

Chapter 2: Neuroplasticity and NEGATIVE Inputs

Neuroplasticity can work both ways – it's not just about positive changes. If your brain is repeatedly exposed to negative experiences, thoughts, or stressors, it can lead to negative changes in your brain's structure and functioning. This is sometimes referred to as "negative plasticity" or "maladaptive plasticity."

Impact on Mental Health:
Negative Thought Patterns: Consistently dwelling on negative thoughts can reinforce them in your brain, leading to a cycle of pessimism and low self-esteem.

Emotional Responses: Chronic stress from negative inputs can lead to increased levels of stress hormones, contributing to anxiety and depression.

Relationships: Negative relationships can create emotional stress and impact your sense of well-being, affecting your overall mental health.

Failures: Repeated failures without effective coping strategies can lead to feelings of hopelessness and decrease your confidence.

Financial Stress: Persistent financial worries can lead to chronic stress, impacting your mental health and overall quality of life.
he impact of prolonged stress on the body and its potential to lead to health issues:

Prolonged mental stress can significantly affect the body's health due to the intricate connection between the mind and body. Chronic stress triggers a series of physiological responses intended to address immediate threats. However, when stress persists over time, these responses can contribute to various health problems.

The immune system weakens, rendering the body more susceptible to illnesses, while the cardiovascular system experiences increased heart rate, elevated blood pressure, and the release of stress hormones that can result in cardiovascular issues.

Digestive problems, muscular tension, respiratory disruptions, and sleep disturbances can also arise. The feedback loop between the mind and body intensifies this impact, potentially leading to the development or exacerbation of conditions such as cardiovascular diseases, autoimmune disorders, gastrointestinal problems, and mental health disorders. Managing chronic stress becomes crucial not only for mental well-being but also for maintaining overall physical health.

Neuroplasticity and POSITIVE Inputs

The latest findings in neuroscience show that our thoughts can actually shape our brains. It's like training a muscle in your brain. When you focus on positive thoughts and experiences, your brain creates new pathways, like building bridges between different parts of your brain. This process is called positive neuroplasticity.

Imagine you're practicing a sport. The more you practice, the better you become. Similarly, when you practice positive thinking, your brain gets better at it. This positive practice strengthens the connections between your brain cells, making you feel happier and more resilient.

The cool thing is that this positive training can help reduce stress, improve your emotions, and make you better at handling challenges. It's like teaching your brain to be more positive, and with time, this training can lead to a lasting change in how you see the world. So, by focusing on positive thoughts, you're actually rewiring your brain for happiness and well-being!

Chapter 3: Neural rewiring through NLP

(Neuro-Linguistic Programming) is a concept that involves using language, thought patterns, and behaviors to positively influence the brain's structure and functioning. NLP is a psychological approach that aims to help individuals create positive changes in their lives by tapping into the brain's neuroplasticity.

There are several NLP techniques that can be utilized for healing and promoting overall health and well-being. Here are a few NLP techniques you can consider:

Anchoring: Anchoring involves associating a specific positive state, emotion, or sensation with a physical touch, sound, or visual cue. You can create anchors for relaxation, confidence, or healing. For example, you can anchor a feeling of calmness by touching your thumb and forefinger together every time you feel relaxed during a deep breathing exercise.

Positive Reframing: This technique involves reframing negative thoughts or beliefs into positive and empowering ones. For healing, you can reframe thoughts about your health challenges into positive statements of healing and progress. For instance, if you think, "I'm always sick," you can reframe it as, "I am taking steps to improve my health and well-being."

Visualizations: Visualization involves creating vivid mental images of positive outcomes. Visualize yourself in a state of vibrant health, engaging in activities you love, and feeling energetic. This can enhance your motivation for taking actions that contribute to your well-being.

Timeline Therapy: This technique involves exploring and reprogramming your internal timeline to release negative emotions, limiting beliefs, and past traumas. It can help you release emotional blocks that might be affecting your health and well-being.

Language Patterns: Pay attention to the language you use to describe your health. Use positive and empowering language when discussing your health and well-being. Instead of saying, "I'm always tired," you can say, "I'm working on boosting my energy and vitality."

Self-Hypnosis: NLP techniques can be combined with self-hypnosis to access your subconscious mind and promote healing suggestions. Guided self-hypnosis sessions focused on healing and well-being can be effective.

Submodalities: Submodalities are the finer distinctions of sensory experience. By working with submodalities, you can change the way you perceive certain experiences. For example, changing the size, brightness, or distance of a mental image related to your health can change your emotional response.

Belief Change Techniques: NLP offers various techniques to shift limiting beliefs that might be hindering your healing process. You can reprogram negative beliefs into positive and supportive ones.

Meta-Model and Milton Model Language Patterns: The Meta-Model helps you challenge and clarify limiting beliefs, while the Milton Model uses vague language to access the subconscious mind and promote positive suggestions.

Remember, NLP techniques are most effective when practiced consistently and with an open mind. It's important to approach them with a genuine intention to improve your health and well-being. If you're new to NLP, you might consider seeking guidance from a trained NLP practitioner or coach who can tailor techniques to your specific needs.

Chapter 4: Anchoring

Anchoring is an NLP technique that can be used for promoting health and well-being. It involves creating a connection between a specific stimulus (anchor) and a desired mental or emotional state. By using anchoring, you can access positive states of mind, relaxation, and motivation to support your health goals. Here's how you can use anchoring for health:

Choose a Positive State: Decide on a specific positive mental or emotional state you want to anchor. It could be a feeling of calmness, motivation to exercise, confidence in your health journey, or a sense of well-being.

Create the Anchor: Choose a physical touch, gesture, or sound that you'll associate with the positive state. For example, you might choose to press your thumb and forefinger together, create a gentle fist, or use a specific word or phrase.

Recall the State: Recreate the positive state vividly in your mind. Remember a time when you felt that state strongly. Engage your senses – visualize the experience, feel the emotions, and imagine the sensations.

Apply the Anchor: At the peak of the positive state, use the chosen anchor. For example, press your thumb and forefinger together firmly. This creates an association between the anchor and the positive state.

Release and Test: Release the anchor and shift your focus to something else. Then, apply the anchor again (thumb and forefinger press) and notice if you can evoke the positive state or feelings associated with it. The anchor should trigger a similar emotional response.

Reinforce: Repeat the anchoring process several times to strengthen the association between the anchor and the positive state. Each time you anchor, make sure you are in the desired mental or emotional state.

Apply to Health Goals: Whenever you're working towards health-related goals, like eating well, exercising, or managing stress, use your anchor. Apply the anchor just before engaging in these activities to activate your desired positive state and motivation.

Generalize: With practice, you can generalize the anchor's effectiveness. This means that over time, the anchor may trigger the positive state even when you're not actively using it.

Remember, anchoring can be a powerful tool, but its effectiveness may vary from person to person. It's important to approach anchoring with an open mind and the intention to enhance your health and well-being. If you find that anchoring is not having the desired effect, you might explore other NLP techniques or seek guidance from a trained practitioner.

Here's an example of how you can use anchoring in an NLP technique for promoting relaxation and stress reduction:

Anchoring for Relaxation:
Choose the Anchor: Decide on a physical touch that you'll associate with a deep state of relaxation. Let's use pressing your thumb and forefinger together for this example.

Create the Positive State: Find a quiet and comfortable place to sit or lie down. Close your eyes and take a few deep, slow breaths. Imagine yourself in a serene and tranquil environment, such as a peaceful beach or a calming forest.

Activate the Anchor: As you immerse yourself in this visualization, press your thumb and forefinger together firmly. Hold them together for a few seconds while fully experiencing the feeling of relaxation and tranquility.

Release the Anchor: Let go of the thumb and forefinger touch and allow your hands to rest comfortably.

Test the Anchor: After a short break, press your thumb and forefinger together again. Notice if you can recall the feelings of relaxation and tranquility that you experienced during the visualization. The anchor should trigger a similar sensation.

Reinforce the Anchor: Repeat this process multiple times over the course of several days. Each time you activate the anchor, focus on deep relaxation and the positive feelings associated with it.

Apply to Stressful Situations: Whenever you encounter a stressful situation, press your thumb and forefinger together to evoke the feelings of relaxation. This can help you access a state of calmness and handle stress more effectively.

Generalize the Anchor: With practice, the anchor can become more effective, and you might find that pressing your thumb and forefinger together automatically triggers a sense of relaxation even without the visualization.

Remember that anchoring is a skill that improves with practice. By consistently using this technique, you can create a strong association between the anchor and the desired state of relaxation, which can be beneficial for managing stress and promoting your overall well-being.

While NLP is based on the idea of influencing the brain's neuroplasticity, it's important to note that the scientific community's consensus on the effectiveness of NLP is mixed. Some individuals find value in NLP techniques, while others may not experience the same level of benefit.
Ultimately, the concept of neural rewiring through NLP emphasizes the potential for individuals to harness their brain's plasticity to create positive changes in their thoughts, emotions, behaviors, and overall well-being. As with any approach, individual experiences may vary, and it's important to explore what works best for you.

Chapter 5: Positive Language

Using positive language involves choosing words and phrases that focus on the good, the possible, and the hopeful. Instead of dwelling on limitations or negative aspects, positive language encourages you to express things in a way that empowers you. For example:
Instead of saying: "I can't do this."
Use positive language: "I will give this my best effort."
Instead of saying: "I'm always so stressed."
Use positive language: "I'm working on finding calm and balance in my life."

Positive language not only changes how you communicate with others but also how you communicate with yourself. It can shape your mindset, boost your confidence, and encourage a more optimistic outlook.

Positive language that you can use to support the process of rewiring your thoughts for better health:

Negative Language: I'm always tired and sluggish.
Positive Language: I'm taking steps to boost my energy and vitality every day.

Negative Language: I'll never lose weight.
Positive Language: I'm committed to making healthy choices that support my weight loss journey.

Negative Language: I can't resist unhealthy food.
Positive Language: I'm making mindful choices that nourish my body and support my well-being.

Negative Language: Exercise is a chore.
Positive Language: I enjoy finding ways to move my body and stay active.

Negative Language: I'm stressed all the time.
Positive Language: I'm learning effective strategies to manage stress and find balance.

Negative Language: I'm prone to sickness.
Positive Language: I'm taking steps to strengthen my immune system and prioritize my health.

Negative Language: I can't break my bad habits.
Positive Language: I'm gradually replacing unhealthy habits with positive ones that benefit my health.

Negative Language: I have no time for self-care.
Positive Language: I'm carving out moments for self-care to nurture my body and mind.

Negative Language: Healthy food is bland and boring.
Positive Language: I'm exploring delicious and nutritious food options that support my well-being.

Negative Language: I'm always stressed about my weight.
Positive Language: I'm focusing on my overall health and well-being, not just my weight.

Negative Language: I'm too old to make changes.
Positive Language: I'm embracing the opportunity to improve my health and well-being at any age.

Negative Language: I'll never find time to exercise.
Positive Language: I'm making exercise a priority and finding creative ways to fit it into my schedule.

Negative Language: I'm not disciplined enough for a healthy lifestyle.
Positive Language: I'm building healthy habits that support my long-term well-being.

Negative Language: I can't cope with my health challenges.
Positive Language: I'm developing resilience and strategies to face my health challenges with determination.

By using positive language, you can reshape your mindset and approach towards health. These affirmations can help you reinforce positive beliefs, cultivate motivation, and inspire actions that contribute to your overall well-being.

Positive language and mindset can have a beneficial impact on a person's overall well-being, especially when dealing with a disease.
 Here are some examples of positive language that can complement medical treatment and support individuals facing health challenges:

Negative Language: I'm a victim of this disease.
Positive Language: I'm facing this challenge with courage and resilience.

Negative Language: This disease defines me.
Positive Language: I am more than my illness, and I'm focused on living a fulfilling life.

Negative Language: I can't do anything because of my condition.
Positive Language: I'm adapting and finding new ways to enjoy life despite my challenges.

Negative Language: I'm helpless in this situation.
Positive Language: I have the power to influence my well-being through my choices and mindset.

Negative Language: I'll never get better.
Positive Language: I'm committed to my healing journey and focusing on progress every day.

Negative Language: My life is limited by this disease.
Positive Language: I'm exploring ways to live my life fully within the scope of my condition.

Negative Language: I'm always in pain.
Positive Language: I'm actively seeking ways to manage my pain and improve my comfort.

Negative Language: I'm burdening my loved ones with my illness.
Positive Language: My loved ones are here to support me, and I'm grateful for their care.

Negative Language: This disease is a punishment.
Positive Language: I'm finding strength and learning valuable lessons through this experience.

Negative Language: My life is over because of this condition.
Positive Language: I'm finding new purpose and meaning in my life, despite the challenges.

Negative Language: I'm afraid of what the future holds.
Positive Language: I'm focusing on the present moment and taking steps to create a positive future.

Negative Language: I'll never enjoy life again.
Positive Language: I'm finding joy in small moments and discovering new sources of happiness.

Negative Language: I'm isolated because of my illness.
Positive Language: I'm reaching out for support and maintaining connections that bring me joy.

Negative Language: I'm defined by my limitations.
Positive Language: I'm embracing my strengths and finding ways to expand my horizons.

Using positive language can help individuals shift their perspective, boost their emotional well-being, and foster a sense of empowerment as they navigate their health challenges. It's important to note that positive language complements medical treatment and can contribute to an overall improved quality of life.

Chapter 6 : Visualisation

Visualizing for good health involves using your imagination to create positive mental images of yourself in a state of optimal well-being. By regularly practicing this visualization, you can potentially support your physical and mental health.

Here's how you can do it:
Find a Quiet Space: Choose a quiet and comfortable place where you won't be disturbed. Sit or lie down in a relaxed position.

Deep Breathing: Take a few deep breaths to relax your body and calm your mind. Inhale deeply through your nose, hold for a moment, and then exhale slowly through your mouth.

Positive Imagery: Close your eyes and start to visualize yourself in a state of vibrant health. Imagine every detail vividly:
> Visualize your body full of vitality, radiating with energy and strength.
> See yourself engaging in activities you enjoy, whether it's walking, exercising, or any other form of movement.
> Imagine your body functioning perfectly, with each organ and system working in harmony.
> Feel a sense of inner peace and calmness permeating your entire being.

Engage Your Senses: As you visualize, engage your senses. Feel the warmth and energy radiating from your body, hear the sounds of your deep and steady breaths, and even imagine the scent of freshness around you.

Add Details: Imagine yourself making healthy choices, like nourishing meals and staying hydrated. Picture yourself enjoying these activities and feeling the benefits.

Positive Affirmations: While visualizing, you can also repeat positive affirmations related to health. For example: "I am grateful for my strong and healthy body," or "I am taking good care of myself."

Emotional Connection: As you continue to visualize, try to evoke positive emotions associated with good health, such as joy, gratitude, and contentment.

Duration: Spend about 5 to 10 minutes on this visualization each day. You can adjust the duration based on what feels comfortable for you.

Consistency: Like any practice, consistency is key. The more you visualize, the more you reinforce positive connections in your brain.

Remember that visualization is a tool to complement a healthy lifestyle, including proper nutrition, exercise, and regular medical check-ups. While it may not replace medical treatments, it can contribute to your overall well-being by promoting a positive mindset and enhancing your motivation to take care of your health. Visualizing when facing a disease can be a powerful tool to complement medical treatment, promote relaxation, and foster a positive mindset. Visualization involves using your imagination to create mental images that evoke positive feelings and thoughts. Here's how you can use visualization to support your well-being while dealing with a disease:

Find a Comfortable Space: Choose a quiet and comfortable place where you won't be disturbed. Sit or lie down in a relaxed position.

Deep Breathing: Begin with a few deep breaths to calm your mind and body. Inhale deeply through your nose, hold for a moment, and exhale slowly through your mouth.

Create a Positive Image: Close your eyes and visualize a calming and healing scene. It could be a peaceful beach, a serene forest, or any place that brings you comfort.

Engage Your Senses: Use your imagination to engage your senses. Feel the warmth of the sun, the gentle breeze, or the soft sand beneath you. Hear the soothing sounds of nature and visualize the colors around you.

Focus on Healing: Imagine a healing light or energy surrounding you, bathing you in positivity and warmth. Visualize this healing energy gently working on the affected areas of your body.

Positive Affirmations: As you visualize, repeat positive affirmations related to your health and well-being. For example, "I am healing and getting stronger every day," or "My body has the power to recover and restore itself."

Visualize Activities: Envision yourself engaging in activities that you love and that promote healing. See yourself taking walks, practicing gentle exercises, or spending quality time with loved ones.

Relaxation and Comfort: Visualize a sense of deep relaxation spreading through your body. Imagine any pain or discomfort easing away, leaving you feeling calm and at ease.

Emotional Connection: As you visualize, focus on the positive emotions that arise. Feel gratitude for the progress you're making and the support you have.

Duration: Spend about 10-15 minutes on this visualization each day, adjusting the duration based on your comfort.

Consistency: Consistent practice can enhance the benefits of visualization. Consider incorporating it into your daily routine.

Visualization is a way to tap into your body's natural ability to relax, heal, and promote well-being. While it's not a substitute for medical treatment, it can contribute to your emotional and mental wellness, helping you feel more empowered and positive as you navigate your health journey.

Chapter 7: Positive Affirmations

Positive affirmations can help you foster a positive mindset and support your journey toward better health. Here are some affirmations that you can use to focus on your well-being:

I am deserving of good health, and I am taking steps to nurture my body and mind.

My body is capable of healing and restoring itself, and I am supporting it on this journey.

Each day, I am getting stronger, healthier, and more vibrant.

I am in control of my health, and I am making choices that nourish and uplift me.

My body is a temple of well-being, and I treat it with love and care.

I am grateful for the progress I'm making on my health journey, no matter how small.

I embrace wellness in all aspects of my life – physical, mental, and emotional.

I am resilient and have the strength to overcome any health challenges that come my way.

I radiate positive energy, and it contributes to my overall health and happiness.

I release any negativity and make room for healing and vitality.

My body is a source of wisdom, and I listen to its signals and needs.

I trust in the healing power within me and align my thoughts with well-being.

Every breath I take nourishes my body with life, energy, and vitality.

I am on a journey of self-care and self-love, and I prioritize my well-being.

Feel free to customise these affirmations to resonate with your personal experiences and health goals. Repeat them daily, write them down, or create a visual reminder to keep them present in your mind.

Positive affirmations can help shift your mindset, boost your motivation, and contribute to a more optimistic outlook on your health and life.

Chapter 8: Deep Breathing

Deep breathing is a simple yet powerful practice that can have profound effects on both mental and physical health. It involves taking slow, deliberate breaths, usually by inhaling deeply through your nose and exhaling slowly through your mouth. Here's how deep breathing benefits both aspects of well-being:

Mental Health Benefits:
Stress Reduction: Deep breathing triggers the body's relaxation response by activating the parasympathetic nervous system. This helps reduce the production of stress hormones like cortisol, leading to a calmer and more relaxed state of mind.

Anxiety Relief: Deep breathing helps regulate the body's fight-or-flight response, reducing feelings of anxiety and panic. It promotes a sense of tranquility and helps you stay grounded in the present moment.
Emotional Balance: Practicing deep breathing can help regulate emotions by promoting mindfulness and enhancing emotional awareness. It allows you to respond to emotions with greater clarity and control.
Improved Focus: Deep breathing increases oxygen flow to the brain, which can enhance cognitive function and improve concentration. It's particularly beneficial for maintaining focus during stressful or challenging situations.
Mind-Body Connection: Deep breathing fosters a connection between the mind and body, promoting mindfulness and reducing racing thoughts. This can help you feel more centered and attuned to your body's needs.

Physical Health Benefits:

Stress Reduction: Deep breathing lowers blood pressure, heart rate, and muscle tension, counteracting the physical effects of stress on the body.

Enhanced Oxygen Intake: Deep breathing allows you to take in more oxygen, improving blood circulation and oxygenating your body's cells. This supports overall cell function and energy production.

Detoxification: Deep breathing promotes lymphatic circulation, aiding the removal of waste and toxins from the body.

Digestion Support: Deep breathing stimulates the parasympathetic nervous system, which aids digestion by promoting relaxation and proper functioning of digestive organs.

Pain Management: By promoting relaxation and reducing tension, deep breathing can help manage pain, especially tension-related pain.

Immune System Support: Reduced stress and improved circulation resulting from deep breathing can positively influence the immune system's functioning.

To practice deep breathing, find a quiet space, sit or lie down in a comfortable position, and focus on your breath. Inhale deeply through your nose for a count of 4, hold for a moment, and exhale slowly through your mouth for a count of 4. Repeat this several times. Regular deep breathing practice, even for just a few minutes a day, can lead to noticeable improvements in both mental and physical well-being over time.

Chapter 9: Self Hypnosis

Self-hypnosis is an NLP technique that involves inducing a state of deep relaxation and focused concentration to access your subconscious mind. It can be a powerful tool for promoting health and well-being by influencing your thoughts, emotions, and behaviors in a positive way.

Preparing for Self-Hypnosis:
Choose a Quiet Space: Find a quiet and comfortable space where you won't be disturbed. Sit or lie down in a relaxed position.

Set an Intention: Decide on a specific health goal or intention you want to work on during your self-hypnosis session. It could be improving your immune system, reducing stress, or cultivating healthy habits.

Use Positive Suggestions: Create a series of positive statements related to your health goal. These statements should be in the present tense and phrased as if you've already achieved your goal. For example, "I am calm and at ease," "I make healthy choices," or "My body is strong and resilient."

Steps for Self-Hypnosis:
Deep Relaxation: Close your eyes and take a few deep breaths to relax. With each exhale, release tension from your body.

Progressive Relaxation: Start from your toes and work your way up, focusing on each part of your body. As you focus on each area, imagine it becoming warm, heavy, and completely relaxed.

Visualize: Imagine a peaceful and calming place, such as a beach or a forest. Visualize yourself there, experiencing a sense of tranquility and well-being.

Repeat Positive Suggestions: Begin repeating your positive suggestions related to your health goal. Say them in a calm and confident voice, either out loud or silently in your mind.

Engage Your Senses: As you repeat the suggestions, engage your senses. Imagine how it feels, looks, sounds, and even smells to have achieved your health goal.

Deepen the State: With each repetition, deepen your state of relaxation. Imagine a staircase with ten steps, and with each step, you descend deeper into relaxation and focus.

Anchor: Create an anchor, such as pressing your thumb and forefinger together, to associate with this state of relaxation and positive suggestions.

Visualize Your Success: Spend some time vividly visualizing yourself enjoying the benefits of your health goal. Imagine yourself engaging in activities that support your well-being.

Count Up: When you're ready to end the session, count slowly from one to five. With each count, tell yourself that you'll become more alert and awake.

Reawaken: Open your eyes, stretch, and reorient yourself to your surroundings.

Benefits of Self-Hypnosis for Health:
Stress Reduction: Self-hypnosis induces a relaxed state that reduces stress and promotes a sense of calm.

Mindset Transformation: It can help you shift negative thought patterns and cultivate a positive mindset toward your health.

Behavior Change: Self-hypnosis can support the adoption of healthy habits by reinforcing positive suggestions.

Immune System Support: By reducing stress, self-hypnosis can indirectly support your immune system's functioning.

Pain Management: It can be used as a complementary technique for managing pain and discomfort.

Remember that regular practice enhances the effectiveness of self-hypnosis. If you're new to self-hypnosis or want personalized guidance, consider using self-hypnosis audio recordings created by professionals or consulting with an experienced NLP practitioner.

Self-hypnosis can be used as a complementary technique to help relieve headache by promoting relaxation, shifting your focus, and influencing your perception of pain.
 Here's how you can use self-hypnosis to potentially alleviate headache discomfort:
Find a Comfortable Space: Choose a quiet and comfortable place where you won't be disturbed. Sit or lie down in a relaxed position.

Deep Relaxation: Close your eyes and take a few deep breaths to relax. With each exhale, release tension from your body.

Progressive Relaxation: Start from your toes and work your way up, focusing on each part of your body. Imagine each area becoming warm, heavy, and free from tension.

Positive Suggestions: Create positive suggestions related to headache relief. These could include statements like, "My head is becoming calm and relaxed," "I am letting go of tension," or "As I relax, my headache fades away."

Visualize Relief: Imagine a soothing, healing light enveloping your head. Visualize the light gently easing away the pain and discomfort.

Deepen the State: With each repetition of positive suggestions, deepen your state of relaxation. Imagine a comforting sensation spreading through your head.

Anchoring: Use a physical touch or gesture as an anchor for your relaxed state. For example, you can gently press your thumb and forefinger together while visualizing relief.

Focus Shifting: Direct your attention away from the pain and onto a calming mental image, such as a serene landscape or a peaceful scene.

Suggest Diminished Pain: Repeat affirmations like, "My headache is easing," "I am feeling more comfortable," or "With each breath, my head feels lighter."

Count Up: When you're ready to end the session, count slowly from one to five. With each count, tell yourself that you'll become more alert and awake.

Reawaken: Open your eyes, stretch, and reorient yourself to your surroundings.

It's important to note that while self-hypnosis can be a useful tool for managing pain, it may not eliminate severe or chronic headaches entirely. It's always recommended to consult with a medical professional if you experience persistent or severe headaches.

Additionally, individual responses to self-hypnosis vary, and its effectiveness may differ from person to person. Regular practice and combining self-hypnosis with other headache management techniques, such as staying hydrated, managing stress, and getting enough rest, can contribute to better results.

Chapter 10: Submodalities

Submodalities are the finer distinctions of sensory experience, and they play a significant role in NLP techniques for promoting health and well-being. By working with submodalities, you can change the way you perceive certain experiences, thoughts, and feelings related to your health. Here's how you can use submodalities in NLP for health:

Changing Perceptions with Submodalities:
Identify a Health Goal: Choose a specific health goal or aspect you want to work on, such as reducing stress, increasing energy, or managing cravings.

Identify the Experience: Think about how you currently experience the situation or feeling related to your health goal. Pay attention to the images, sounds, feelings, and self-talk associated with it.

Submodalities Exploration:
> Visual Submodalities: Experiment with the visual aspects of the experience. For example, change the brightness, size, distance, or color of the mental image associated with your health goal.
>
> Auditory Submodalities: Modify the sounds associated with your health goal. Adjust the volume, tone, or location of any internal dialogue or self-talk related to your health.
>
> Kinesthetic Submodalities: Change the feelings and sensations associated with the experience. Adjust the intensity, location, or movement of any physical sensations or emotions related to your health goal.

Olfactory and Gustatory Submodalities: If applicable, consider any smells or tastes associated with your health goal. Imagine altering these sensations.

Positive Submodalities: Choose the submodalities that create the most positive and empowering experience for your health goal. This might involve making images brighter, sounds more motivating, or feelings more soothing.

Mental Rehearsal: Visualize yourself achieving your health goal using the newly adjusted submodalities. Imagine every detail vividly, engaging your senses.

Anchor the Positive Experience: Create an anchor, such as pressing your thumb and forefinger together, while fully experiencing the positive submodalities. This anchors the empowering experience.

Apply the Anchor: Whenever you're working towards your health goal, activate the anchor. Use the anchor as a trigger to access the positive submodalities and reinforce the empowering experience.

Benefits of Submodalities for Health:
Mindset Transformation: Changing submodalities can shift your perception of health-related experiences from negative to positive, leading to a more optimistic mindset.

Enhanced Motivation: By adjusting submodalities to make the experience more motivating and rewarding, you can increase your motivation to engage in healthy behaviors.

Reduced Stress: Altering the sensory aspects of stressful thoughts or situations can reduce the emotional charge and stress response.

Increased Resilience: Working with submodalities can enhance your resilience by changing how you perceive challenges and setbacks related to your health.

Better Self-Talk: Adjusting the auditory submodalities of self-talk can help you cultivate a more supportive inner dialogue related to your health goals.

Remember that submodalities are highly individual, so what works best for one person may not be the same for another. Experiment with different submodalities and find the combinations that resonate most with you and support your health journey. If you find it challenging to work with submodalities on your own, consider seeking guidance from an experienced NLP practitioner.

Chapter 11: Belief Change

Belief change techniques in NLP are powerful tools that can help you shift limiting beliefs and replace them with empowering ones, thereby supporting your health and well-being. Here are some belief change techniques you can use:

Belief Elicitation:
> Identify a specific limiting belief related to your health, such as "I can't lose weight" or "I'll always have low energy."
> Write down the belief and notice how it makes you feel.
> Reflect on where this belief might have come from and why you've held onto it.

Reframing:
> Examine the limiting belief from different perspectives. Ask yourself if there's another way to interpret the situation.
> Find evidence that contradicts the limiting belief. For instance, recall times when you did experience positive changes in your health.
> Reframe the belief into a more empowering statement. For example, change "I can't lose weight" to "I am capable of making healthy choices."

Anchoring Empowering Beliefs:
> Choose a physical anchor (e.g., pressing your thumb and forefinger together) that you associate with feeling empowered.
> Recall a time when you felt confident and empowered in your health.
> While experiencing that memory, activate the anchor. This links the positive feeling to the anchor.

Future Pacing:

- Imagine your life with the new empowering belief fully integrated.
- Visualize how your health and well-being have improved with this new belief in place.
- Engage your senses to make the visualization vivid and compelling.

Timeline Therapy for Beliefs:
- Use the timeline visualization technique to go back to the origin of the limiting belief.
- Examine the events that led to the formation of the belief and their impact on you.
- Reframe the memories with a positive perspective and new insights.

Submodalities for Beliefs:
- Think about the limiting belief and notice the submodalities of the mental image, self-talk, and feelings associated with it.
- Adjust the submodalities to make the limiting belief less intense and the empowering belief more vivid and compelling.

Positive Affirmations:
- Create positive affirmations that counteract the limiting belief.
- Repeat these affirmations daily, with conviction and belief, to reinforce the new empowering mindset.

Modeling Successful Beliefs:
- Identify people who have achieved the health and well-being you desire.
- Study their beliefs and behaviors related to health.
- Model their empowering beliefs and adapt them to your own situation.

Remember that changing beliefs takes time and consistent effort. It's essential to be patient with yourself and practice these techniques regularly. Working with an experienced NLP practitioner can provide personalized guidance and support in the belief change process. Additionally, be open to monitoring your progress and adjusting your techniques as needed to align with your evolving health goals.

Chapter :12 Meta Modal & Milton Modal

The Meta-Model and Milton Model are linguistic patterns used in NLP to communicate more effectively, either by getting specific information (Meta-Model) or inducing a trance-like state for positive suggestion (Milton Model). These patterns can be applied to health-related conversations to promote well-being and positive change. Here's how you can use both models in the context of health:

Meta-Model Language Patterns for Health:
Challenge Limiting Assumptions:
- If someone expresses a limiting belief about their health, ask, "How do you know that's true?"
- This encourages them to examine the evidence supporting their belief and potentially opens up new perspectives.

Specify Vague Statements:
- If someone says, "I always feel tired," ask, "Always? Can you think of a time when you didn't feel tired?"
- This helps them refine their language, encouraging a more accurate description of their health experiences.

Identify Cause-Effect Relationships:
- If someone attributes their health issues to external factors, ask, "How does [factor] cause [issue]?"
- This prompts them to clarify the causal link between their beliefs and their health experiences.

Challenge Universal Quantifiers:
- If someone says, "Everyone gets sick during winter," ask, "Is there really no one who doesn't get sick?"
- This challenges broad generalizations, inviting them to consider exceptions to their beliefs.

Milton Model Language Patterns for Health:

Utilize Open-Ended Suggestions:
> Use vague language to induce a relaxed state and open-mindedness. For example, "As you allow yourself to relax, you might find new ways to support your well-being."

Embedded Commands for Positive Change:
> Embed positive suggestions within sentences. For instance, "You can notice how your body is becoming more balanced and healthy every day."

Metaphors and Analogies:
> Share metaphors or stories that relate to health improvement. Metaphors engage the subconscious mind. For example, "Just as a garden flourishes with care, your body thrives when you nurture it."

Presuppositions:
> Use presuppositions to guide the listener's focus. "As you continue to explore different ways to enhance your well-being, you may find yourself naturally drawn to healthier choices."

Double Binds:
> Present options that both lead to positive outcomes. "Would you prefer to feel more relaxed now, or would you rather enjoy this feeling of calmness a little later?"

Lack of Referential Index:
> Use statements that are intentionally vague, allowing the listener to interpret them in a way that serves their health goals. "You might discover ways to boost your energy that surprise you."

Remember that using these language patterns ethically and with genuine intention is crucial. While the Meta-Model encourages precision and clarity, the Milton Model focuses on creating positive shifts in mindset. Incorporating these patterns into health-related conversations can enhance communication, promote well-being, and facilitate positive change.

The Meta-Model can be applied to gain clarity in the context of NLP and health:

Challenge Generalizations:
>Statement: "I can never stick to a healthy routine."
>Meta-Model Response: "Are there specific instances where you've struggled with a healthy routine? Is it accurate to say 'never'?"

Deletion of Information:
>Statement: "I feel overwhelmed."
>Meta-Model Response: "What specifically is overwhelming you? Can you identify the factors contributing to this feeling?"

Distortion of Meaning:
>Statement: "I'll always be overweight."
>Meta-Model Response: "In what situations have you felt overweight? Can you think of times when your weight hasn't been an issue?"

Mind Reading:
>Statement: "People think I'm not disciplined enough to be healthy."
>Meta-Model Response: "How do you know what others think about your discipline? Have they explicitly shared these opinions?"

Cause-Effect:
>Statement: "Stress from work is causing my health problems."
>Meta-Model Response: "How does work-related stress directly impact your health problems? Are there any other factors contributing?"

Lost Performative:
> Statement: "It's hard for everyone to eat healthily."
> Meta-Model Response: "Who specifically finds it hard to eat healthily? Can you provide examples of individuals who have successfully maintained a healthy diet?"

Nominalization:
> Statement: "I struggle with anxiety."
> Meta-Model Response: "What does 'anxiety' mean to you? Can you describe the specific thoughts, sensations, or situations that trigger your anxiety?"

Comparison:
> Statement: "I'm not as fit as my friends."
> Meta-Model Response: "Which friends are you comparing yourself to? In what specific ways do you feel less fit?"

Applying the Meta-Model to health-related statements can uncover underlying assumptions, clarify vague language, and encourage individuals to explore their health perceptions more deeply. This can lead to greater self-awareness, more accurate problem-solving, and a clearer understanding of their health goals and challenges.

The Milton Model is a set of language patterns used in NLP to induce a trance-like state, inspire creativity, and facilitate positive changes in mindset. When applied to the context of health, the Milton Model can encourage motivation, relaxation, and a more open and receptive attitude towards well-being. Here's how the Milton Model can be used for inspiration in NLP health:

Embedded Commands:
> Statement: "As you explore ways to improve your health, you might find yourself naturally drawn to healthier choices."
> How It Works: The embedded command "explore ways to improve your health" can inspire action while bypassing resistance.

Metaphorical Language:
: Statement: "Just like a river flows steadily, your journey to better health can follow a smooth and natural path."
: How It Works: Metaphorical language engages the subconscious mind, fostering a sense of calmness and flow in the pursuit of health.

Presuppositions:
: Statement: "As you continue to learn about different aspects of well-being, you may find yourself integrating these insights effortlessly."
: How It Works: The presupposition that the listener will "continue to learn" and "integrate insights effortlessly" encourages a positive attitude towards ongoing health improvement.

Vague Language:
: Statement: "Sometimes, people discover unique ways to nurture their health and well-being."
: How It Works: The vague language allows the listener's mind to fill in the specifics, encouraging creativity and open-mindedness.

Double Binds:
: Statement: "Would you prefer to start feeling more energetic now, or would you rather enjoy this boost of vitality a little later?"
: How It Works: The double bind offers two positive options, inspiring the listener to embrace increased energy levels.

Unspecified Verbs:
: Statement: "As you breathe deeply, your body naturally begins to relax and recharge."
: How It Works: The unspecified verb "breathe deeply" encourages the listener to engage in calming actions.

Preserving Freedom:
> Statement: "You can choose to embrace health-enhancing habits whenever it feels right for you."
> How It Works: Preserving the listener's choice empowers them to take charge of their health on their terms.

Applying the Milton Model in NLP health conversations can help individuals tap into their inner motivation, create a positive mindset, and foster a receptive attitude towards adopting healthier habits. It encourages the mind to explore possibilities and engage in positive changes that contribute to overall well-being.

PART 2

HAPPINESS

Discovering Bliss through NLP

"Harmonising Life's Pleasures"

Happiness is a positive emotional state characterized by feelings of joy, contentment, and well-being. It is a subjective and multifaceted experience that can encompass various emotions, thoughts, and sensations. While the specific nature of happiness can vary from person to person, it generally involves a sense of satisfaction, pleasure, and a positive outlook on life.
Happiness goes beyond fleeting moments of pleasure and extends to a more sustained sense of fulfillment. It's often influenced by factors such as personal values, relationships, achievements, experiences, and one's overall perspective on life. Happiness is not a constant state but rather a fluctuating emotional landscape that can be influenced by both internal factors, such as mindset and attitudes, and external circumstances.

Cultivating happiness involves nurturing positive emotions, practicing gratitude, engaging in activities that bring joy, fostering meaningful connections, and adopting a positive mindset. It's important to note that happiness is a complex and individualised experience, and what brings happiness to one person might differ from another. Ultimately, the pursuit of happiness is a central aspect of human existence, guiding individuals in their quest for a meaningful and fulfilling life.

1. How to be Happy

Happiness is a complex and subjective emotion that can be influenced by various factors. While there's no one-size-fits-all formula for happiness, here are some general principles and strategies that may help you cultivate happiness in your life:

Positive Mindset: Cultivate a positive outlook on life by focusing on your strengths, accomplishments, and things you're grateful for. Practice mindfulness to stay present and reduce negative rumination.

Healthy Relationships: Build and nurture strong, supportive relationships with friends, family, and loved ones. Positive social interactions and connections are crucial for emotional well-being.

Physical Well-being: Take care of your body through regular exercise, proper nutrition, and sufficient sleep. Physical health can have a significant impact on your overall mood and happiness.

Engaging Activities: Engage in activities that bring you joy, whether it's pursuing hobbies, spending time in nature, creating art, or participating in sports. Doing things you love can boost your mood and provide a sense of accomplishment.

Setting Goals: Set realistic and meaningful goals for yourself. Working towards achieving your goals can give you a sense of purpose and satisfaction.

Practice Gratitude: Regularly express gratitude for the positive aspects of your life. Keeping a gratitude journal or simply reflecting on the good things can increase feelings of happiness.

Helping Others: Engage in acts of kindness and contribute to your community. Helping others can create a sense of fulfillment and enhance your own well-being.

Limit Materialism: While material possessions can provide temporary satisfaction, focusing excessively on material wealth often doesn't lead to lasting happiness. Shift your focus towards experiences and relationships instead.

Manage Stress: Develop effective stress-management techniques, such as deep breathing, meditation, yoga, or other relaxation methods. Managing stress can contribute to a more positive outlook.

Seek Professional Help: If you're struggling with persistent feelings of unhappiness, anxiety, or depression, consider seeking guidance from a mental health professional. Therapy or counseling can provide valuable tools for managing your emotions.

Embrace Challenges: View challenges as opportunities for growth and learning rather than as insurmountable obstacles. Developing resilience can lead to greater happiness in the long run.

Practice Self-compassion: Treat yourself with the same kindness and understanding that you would offer to a friend. Be patient with yourself and avoid harsh self-criticism.

Remember that happiness is a journey and can vary from person to person. It's okay to have moments of unhappiness, as they are a natural part of life. Strive for a balance between pursuing happiness and accepting that it's normal to experience a range of emotions.

Here are some simple tips to be happy:
Think Positive: Focus on good things and be thankful for them.

Be with Loved Ones: Spend time with family and friends who make you feel good.

Take Care of Yourself: Eat well, exercise, and sleep enough to feel strong.

Do Fun Stuff: Enjoy activities you like, like hobbies or being outdoors.

Have Goals: Work towards things you want to achieve for a sense of purpose.

Say Thank You: Be grateful for the good things in your life.

Help Others: Doing nice things for others can make you feel good too.

Don't Just Want Stuff: Don't focus too much on things you can buy. Experiences matter more.

Deal with Stress: Find ways to relax, like taking deep breaths or meditating.

Get Help if Needed: If you feel really sad, it's okay to talk to someone who can help, like a counselor.

Learn from Hard Times: Challenges can help you grow and become happier in the end.

Be Kind to Yourself: Treat yourself nicely and don't be too hard on yourself.

Remember, happiness is a journey, and it's okay to feel different emotions sometimes. Just try these things to feel happier in general.

2. Unhappiness

There are various factors that can contribute to feelings of unhappiness. Here are some common reasons:

Stress and Pressure: High levels of stress from work, school, relationships, or other responsibilities can lead to unhappiness. Constant pressure can make you feel overwhelmed and exhausted.

Negative Thinking: Constantly focusing on negative thoughts and self-criticism can contribute to unhappiness. Pessimistic attitudes can color your perception of situations and the world.

Lack of Fulfillment: Not pursuing activities or goals that bring you a sense of purpose and accomplishment can lead to feelings of emptiness and unhappiness.

Loneliness and Isolation: Lack of meaningful connections with others and feelings of isolation can cause unhappiness. Humans are social creatures, and social interactions are important for well-being.

Unresolved Issues: Unresolved conflicts, past traumas, and emotional baggage can continue to affect your happiness if not addressed.

Comparison: Constantly comparing yourself to others, especially on social media, can make you feel inadequate and unhappy.

Unhealthy Lifestyle: Poor eating habits, lack of exercise, and inadequate sleep can negatively impact your physical well-being, which in turn affects your mood.

Lack of Self-Care: Neglecting self-care and not taking time for yourself can lead to burnout and unhappiness.

Financial Stress: Money problems, debt, and financial instability can cause a great deal of stress and unhappiness.

Uncertainty and Change: Fear of the unknown and major life changes can lead to anxiety and unhappiness.

Unrealistic Expectations: Setting impossibly high standards for yourself or others can result in constant disappointment and unhappiness.

Health Issues: Physical health problems, chronic pain, or serious illnesses can impact your overall well-being and lead to unhappiness.

Lack of Meaning: Feeling that your life lacks meaning or purpose can lead to a sense of emptiness and unhappiness.

Grief and Loss: Experiencing the loss of a loved one or going through a significant life change, like a breakup or job loss, can cause feelings of grief and unhappiness.

Negative Environment: Being in an environment that's toxic, unsupportive, or unfulfilling can contribute to unhappiness.

Mental Health Issues: Conditions like depression, anxiety, or other mental health disorders can have a significant impact on your mood and overall happiness.

It's important to remember that everyone's experience of unhappiness is unique, and multiple factors can interact to influence your emotional state. If you're consistently feeling unhappy and struggling to cope, consider seeking support from friends, family, or a mental health professional.

3. Vices : The cause of Our Unhappiness

Vices are behaviors or habits that are considered morally wrong or harmful, and they can indeed contribute to feelings of unhappiness. Engaging in vices can lead to negative consequences that impact both your physical and mental well-being.
Few ways in which vices can contribute to unhappiness:
Health Effects: Many vices, such as smoking, excessive alcohol consumption, or drug abuse, can have serious negative effects on your physical health. These health issues can cause pain, discomfort, and reduce your overall quality of life.

Emotional Toll: Vices often provide temporary relief or pleasure, but they can lead to guilt, shame, and emotional distress in the long run. For example, overeating unhealthy foods may provide comfort temporarily, but it can lead to negative emotions and self-esteem issues over time.

Strained Relationships: Engaging in vices can strain relationships with loved ones and friends. The behavior itself and the consequences that arise from it can lead to conflicts and a sense of isolation.

Financial Burden: Many vices, such as excessive spending or gambling, can lead to financial problems, which can cause stress and anxiety, contributing to unhappiness.

Loss of Control: Vices can become addictive, making it difficult to control your actions. This loss of control can lead to a sense of powerlessness and unhappiness.

Negative Self-Image: Vices often contradict your values and goals, leading to a negative self-perception. This can erode your self-esteem and happiness.

Impact on Personal Goals: Engaging in vices can divert your focus from pursuing meaningful goals, leading to a lack of fulfillment and happiness.

Recognizing and addressing vices can be a challenging but important step toward improving your overall well-being. By reducing or eliminating vices from your life, you can create space for healthier habits and behaviors that contribute to a happier and more fulfilling life. If you're struggling with vices and their impact on your happiness, consider seeking support from friends, family, or professionals who can provide guidance and assistance.

4. Emotional Toll

Healing emotional toll and cultivating happiness through Neuro-Linguistic Programming (NLP) involves using techniques and strategies to reframe negative thought patterns, manage emotions, and create positive change in your mindset.

Use NLP principles to promote emotional healing and happiness: Identify Negative Patterns: Begin by recognizing negative thought patterns, limiting beliefs, and emotions that are contributing to your emotional toll. NLP encourages self-awareness as a first step toward change.

Reframe Negative Thoughts: Use NLP techniques like reframing to shift your perspective on challenging situations. Instead of dwelling on the negative aspects, find alternative interpretations that empower you and lead to more positive emotions.

Anchoring: Create positive anchors by associating specific physical sensations or actions with positive emotions. This can help you access feelings of happiness whenever you need them. For example, touch your thumb and index finger together when you feel joyful, and over time, this touch can trigger that feeling.

Visualize Success: NLP often involves visualization techniques. Imagine yourself overcoming challenges and experiencing happiness. Visualizing positive outcomes can help rewire your brain for optimism.

Timeline Therapy: This NLP technique involves working with your personal timeline to release negative emotions associated with past events. By changing how you remember and feel about those events, you can promote emotional healing.

Language Use: Be mindful of the language you use both internally and externally. Replace negative self-talk with positive affirmations and empowering language. This can shape your mindset and emotions.

Submodalities: NLP emphasizes the use of sensory experiences. Identify the submodalities (sensory details) of your negative emotions, and then experiment with changing them to alter how you experience those emotions.

Goal Setting: Set clear and achievable goals for your emotional healing and happiness. NLP techniques can help you create a roadmap for personal growth and positive change.

Pattern Interrupt: Interrupt negative patterns by consciously choosing different behaviors, thoughts, or actions when you notice yourself slipping into negative emotions. This can break the cycle and redirect your mind toward more positive feelings.

Practice Mindfulness: Incorporate mindfulness techniques into your routine to stay present and aware of your thoughts and emotions. Mindfulness can help you manage negative emotions and cultivate a calmer, more contented mindset.

Seek Professional Guidance: While NLP techniques can be powerful, seeking guidance from a trained NLP practitioner or mental health professional can provide personalized support and guidance tailored to your specific needs.

Remember that healing and cultivating happiness is a process that takes time and consistent effort. NLP offers tools to assist you, but it's important to be patient with yourself and open to trying different techniques until you find what works best for you.

An example of how you might use NLP techniques to heal emotional toll and promote happiness:

Let's say you often feel anxious and stressed in social situations, leading to unhappiness and avoidance of social events. You want to change this pattern using NLP:

Identify Negative Pattern: Recognize that you tend to feel anxious and stressed in social situations, and this leads to avoiding them, causing you to miss out on potential happiness and connections.

Reframe Negative Thoughts: When you think about social situations, instead of focusing on what could go wrong, reframe your thoughts to focus on the positive aspects. For instance, remind yourself that social events are opportunities to meet interesting people and have enjoyable conversations.

Anchoring: Create a positive anchor by gently pressing your thumb and index finger together while you're feeling relaxed and happy. Practice this anchoring technique regularly, associating the physical touch with positive emotions.

Visualize Success: Close your eyes and visualize yourself at a social event feeling confident and engaged in conversations. See yourself enjoying the company of others and having a good time.

Submodalities: Identify the sensory details of your anxious feelings. Change them by imagining the negative feelings as smaller, distant, or less intense. Replace the mental images and sounds associated with stress with images and sounds of calmness.

Language Use: Replace thoughts like "I'm always anxious in social situations" with affirmations like "I am becoming more comfortable and confident in social settings."

Goal Setting: Set a goal to attend a small social gathering and have one positive interaction. Break the goal down into manageable steps, and celebrate your progress along the way.

Pattern Interrupt: When you notice feelings of anxiety creeping in before a social event, use a pattern interrupt by taking a deep breath and telling yourself, "I am in control of my emotions. I choose to feel confident and at ease."

Practice Mindfulness: Before attending a social event, take a few moments to focus on your breath and bring your attention to the present moment. This can help reduce anxious thoughts and ground you in the here and now.

Seek Professional Guidance: If your social anxiety persists, consider seeking support from an NLP practitioner or a mental health professional who can provide more tailored guidance.

By applying these NLP techniques, you can gradually shift your mindset, manage your anxiety, and approach social situations with more confidence and happiness. Remember that consistent practice and patience are key to making positive changes.

5. Jealously

Jealousy can indeed contribute to feelings of unhappiness and negatively impact relationships. Overcoming jealousy involves self-awareness, self-reflection, and adopting healthier perspectives and behaviors.

The steps you can take to address and cure jealousy:
Recognize and Acknowledge: Acknowledge that you're experiencing jealousy. Understand that it's a normal emotion, but it's important to address it in a constructive way.

Identify Triggers: Identify the situations, events, or people that trigger your jealousy. Knowing your triggers can help you better understand the underlying causes of your feelings.

Self-Reflect: Explore the reasons behind your jealousy. Is it rooted in insecurities, past experiences, or fears? Self-reflection can help you uncover the deeper emotions driving your jealousy.

Challenge Negative Thoughts: Question and challenge the negative thoughts and assumptions that fuel your jealousy. Consider whether your fears are based on evidence or assumptions.

Practice Empathy: Put yourself in the other person's shoes and try to understand their perspective. This can help you see things from a more balanced viewpoint.

Communicate Openly: If your jealousy is related to a specific relationship, have an open and honest conversation with the person involved. Express your feelings without blaming or accusing them.

Focus on Self-Improvement: Invest time and energy in your personal growth and self-esteem. When you feel better about yourself, you're less likely to feel threatened by others.

Celebrate Your Achievements: Focus on your own accomplishments and strengths instead of comparing yourself to others. This can boost your self-confidence and reduce jealousy.

Practice Gratitude: Cultivate gratitude for what you have rather than focusing on what others have. Counting your blessings can shift your focus away from jealousy.

Limit Social Media: Limit your exposure to social media if it triggers feelings of jealousy. Remember that people often present a curated version of their lives online, which may not reflect reality.

Develop Trust: Work on building and maintaining trust in your relationships. Trust is essential for overcoming jealousy.

Establish Boundaries: Clearly define boundaries in your relationships to reduce misunderstandings and potential triggers for jealousy.

Seek Support: If jealousy is causing significant distress, consider seeking support from a therapist or counselor. They can help you explore the underlying causes and develop coping strategies.

Practice Mindfulness: Engage in mindfulness practices to stay present and manage your emotions. Mindfulness can help you observe your feelings without being overwhelmed by them.

Cultivate Self-Compassion: Be kind to yourself and recognize that everyone has moments of jealousy. Treat yourself with the same understanding you'd offer a friend.

Remember that overcoming jealousy takes time and effort. Be patient with yourself and celebrate your progress along the way. By addressing the root causes of your jealousy and adopting healthier behaviors and attitudes, you can work toward a happier and more fulfilling mindset.

6. People's Opinion

Dealing with unnecessary opinions from others and finding ways to manage your emotional response can indeed contribute to greater happiness. While NLP techniques can be helpful, it's important to note that NLP isn't a direct "cure" for external opinions but rather a tool to help you change your internal responses and mindset.

Try to apply these NLP principles to handle unnecessary opinions:
Awareness: Recognize that you have the power to control your reactions to other people's opinions. Be aware of your emotions and how they're triggered by external input.

Refocus on Your Values: Remind yourself of your own values, goals, and priorities. When you have a strong sense of self and direction, others' opinions matter less.

Reframe Negative Thoughts: Use NLP reframing techniques to change your perception of others' opinions. Instead of feeling upset, consider how their input might offer a different perspective or even an opportunity for growth.

Practice Anchoring: Create a mental anchor that you can activate when you encounter unnecessary opinions. This anchor could be a calming word or phrase that helps you stay centered.

Limit Impact: Visualize a protective barrier around you that prevents unnecessary opinions from affecting your emotional state. Imagine these opinions bouncing off harmlessly.

Language Mastery: Use NLP language techniques to frame conversations in a positive and empowering way. For instance, use language that acknowledges the other person's input but maintains your own perspective.

Build Confidence: Use NLP techniques to boost your self-confidence and self-esteem. When you're more confident in yourself, the impact of others' opinions diminishes.

Practice Mindfulness: Engage in mindfulness exercises to stay present and non-judgmentally observe your reactions to others' opinions. This can help you detach from the emotional response.

Focus on Empathy: Use NLP to cultivate empathy toward the person offering the opinion. Understanding their perspective can make their input feel less personal.

Respond, Don't React: Instead of immediately reacting emotionally, take a moment to respond thoughtfully. NLP can help you control your emotional reactions and choose a constructive response.

Create Positive Associations: Use anchoring techniques to associate positive emotions with instances when you handle unnecessary opinions with grace and resilience.

Seek Support: If dealing with unnecessary opinions becomes overwhelming, consider seeking support from an NLP practitioner or therapist. They can provide personalized guidance.

Remember, the goal isn't to completely disregard others' opinions but to manage your emotional response to them and prioritize your own well-being. NLP techniques can help you shift your mindset and emotions, but they also require consistent practice and patience to be effective.

Here's an example of how you might use NLP techniques to handle unnecessary opinions from others:

Situation: You're pursuing a creative project, such as writing a novel, and someone gives you unsolicited negative feedback that makes you feel discouraged.

NLP Approach:
Awareness: Recognise that the negative feedback triggered an emotional response. Understand that their opinion is just one perspective.

Refocus on Values: Remind yourself of your passion for your creative project and the fulfillment it brings you. Focus on your own goals and what matters most to you.

Reframe Negative Thoughts: Instead of feeling discouraged, reframe the feedback as an opportunity to improve your work. Consider that every piece of feedback, even negative, can help you refine your creative process.

Anchor a Calm State: Recall a time when you felt confident and calm. As you remember that moment, gently press your thumb and index finger together. Use this anchor to bring back those feelings when you encounter unnecessary opinions.

Language Mastery: When responding, acknowledge the feedback without becoming defensive. Say something like, "Thank you for your input. I'm still in the process of creating and refining this project."

Mindful Detachment: Practice mindfulness by observing your emotional reaction without judgment. Imagine the emotions as passing clouds in the sky, gradually moving away.

Focus on Empathy: Put yourself in the other person's shoes. Understand that their opinion might be influenced by their own experiences and preferences.

Respond, Don't React: Instead of reacting impulsively, take a deep breath before responding. Choose your words thoughtfully to maintain your composure.

Create Positive Associations: After handling the situation with grace, activate your calming anchor. Over time, this anchor can become associated with handling opinions gracefully.

Seek Internal Validation: Remind yourself that your own satisfaction and growth are more important than seeking approval from others.

By applying these NLP techniques, you can transform your emotional response to unnecessary opinions. Remember that practice is key, and over time, you'll become more skilled at managing your reactions and maintaining your own sense of happiness and fulfillment.

7. Lean How Not to Care

Learning how not to care too much about others' opinions or external validation can be liberating and contribute to your overall well-being.
Some strategies to help you navigate this process:
Self-Reflection: Understand why you value others' opinions so much. Is it due to insecurity, a need for approval, or a fear of judgment? Identifying the root cause can help you address it more effectively.

Develop Self-Confidence: Work on building your self-esteem and confidence. When you believe in yourself and your abilities, external opinions hold less sway over your emotions.

Know Your Values: Clarify your own values, priorities, and goals. When you have a strong sense of self and direction, external opinions matter less.

Set Boundaries: Establish clear boundaries regarding what opinions you allow to affect you. Not every opinion needs to be given equal weight.

Focus on Self-Approval: Learn to validate yourself and your choices. Seek internal validation by acknowledging your achievements and growth.

Practice Mindfulness: Engage in mindfulness exercises to stay present and observe your thoughts and emotions without judgment. This can help you detach from external opinions.

Challenge Assumptions: Question the validity of the opinions you're concerned about. Are they based on facts or assumptions?

Learning to differentiate between the two can help you prioritize what truly matters.

Practice Letting Go: Visualize releasing the burden of caring too much about others' opinions. Imagine the weight lifting off your shoulders as you embrace your own path.

Affirmations: Use positive affirmations to remind yourself of your self-worth and the importance of your own perspective.

Surround Yourself with Positivity: Spend time with people who uplift and support you. Positive influences can help counterbalance negative opinions.

Limit Exposure: If certain environments or social media platforms trigger excessive concern for others' opinions, consider reducing your exposure.

Shift Focus Inward: Channel your energy into personal growth, hobbies, and activities that bring you joy. When you're focused on your own journey, external opinions become less central.

Practice Gratitude: Cultivate gratitude for who you are and what you have. Focusing on the positive aspects of your life can minimize the impact of external negativity.

Remind Yourself of Imperfection: Understand that nobody is perfect, and everyone receives both positive and negative feedback. It's okay to make mistakes and learn from them.

Seek Professional Help: If caring too much about others' opinions becomes overwhelming, consider seeking guidance from a therapist or counselor who can provide personalized strategies.

Remember, it's not about completely disregarding others' opinions, but finding a healthy balance between valuing input and prioritizing your own well-being. Over time, practicing these strategies can help you cultivate a stronger sense of self and emotional resilience.

An example of how to apply the strategies for learning how not to care too much about others' opinions:
Imagine you're considering a career change, but you're worried about what your friends and family will think. You find that their potential opinions are causing you stress and uncertainty.

To address this, you could start by reflecting on why their opinions matter so much to you. You realize that you often seek approval to avoid criticism. Building self-confidence becomes your priority, so you set out to list your achievements and acknowledge your strengths. This helps you establish a foundation of self-worth.

Knowing your values, you remind yourself that your career decision is based on what aligns with your goals and aspirations. You practice mindfulness to stay focused on your own path, and you challenge assumptions about others' judgments by questioning if they're grounded in reality or just assumptions.

To practice letting go of excessive concern, you visualize shedding the weight of others' opinions like a heavy coat. You also limit exposure to negative influences, surrounding yourself with friends who support your decisions. You shift your focus inward by dedicating time to hobbies you're passionate about, which boosts your self-esteem.

Through positive affirmations, you reaffirm your belief in your ability to make choices that benefit you. You remind yourself that perfection isn't necessary and that everyone makes mistakes. As you embrace your imperfections, you find a renewed sense of self-acceptance.

By applying these strategies, you gradually lessen the impact of others' opinions on your well-being. While you still value input from others, you've learned not to let it overshadow your own convictions and goals. As you continue to practice these techniques, you discover a newfound sense of confidence and contentment in being true to yourself.

8. Building Confidence

Building confidence through Neuro-Linguistic Programming (NLP) involves using techniques to rewire your mindset, overcome limiting beliefs, and cultivate a strong sense of self-assurance.
Use NLP principles to boost your confidence:
Positive Self-Talk: Replace negative self-talk with positive affirmations. Use empowering statements that reinforce your self-worth and abilities. Repeat these affirmations regularly to create a positive internal dialogue.

Visualization: Imagine yourself confidently achieving your goals. Create vivid mental images of success, feeling the emotions associated with accomplishment. This helps your subconscious mind accept your confidence.

Anchoring: Create a physical anchor (like touching your thumb and index finger together) associated with a confident state. Activate this anchor whenever you need a confidence boost, and recall moments when you felt confident.

Resourceful States: Recall moments from your past when you felt confident. Remember the sensations, thoughts, and emotions of those times. Replicate those feelings in current situations.

Reframe Limiting Beliefs: Identify and challenge limiting beliefs that hold you back. Replace "I can't" with "I can." Use NLP techniques to shift your perspective and see challenges as opportunities for growth.

Use Powerful Language: Choose confident and assertive language in your communication. Use words that express certainty, commitment, and authority.

Model Confidence: Identify people you admire for their confidence. Observe their behavior, body language, and communication style. Incorporate these aspects into your own demeanor.

Develop a Confident Posture: Use NLP to adjust your body language. Stand tall, make eye contact, and project confidence through your posture.

Change Submodalities: Alter the sensory aspects of your memories to enhance your confidence. Make positive memories more vibrant by increasing brightness, volume, and vividness.

Break Down Goals: Use NLP techniques to break down larger goals into smaller, achievable steps. Successfully accomplishing these steps boosts your confidence incrementally.

Utilize Affiliation: Spend time with confident and positive individuals. Surrounding yourself with people who exude confidence can positively influence your own mindset.

Embrace Failure: Use NLP to reframe failures as learning experiences. Change your perception of setbacks from negative to valuable opportunities for growth.

Future Pacing: Visualize yourself confidently handling future situations. Mentally rehearse scenarios where you're confident, successful, and in control.

Mindfulness and Acceptance: Practice mindfulness to stay present and non-judgmentally observe your thoughts and emotions. Accept yourself and your experiences without self-criticism.

Seek Professional Help: If self-doubt significantly hinders your confidence, consider seeking support from an NLP practitioner or therapist for personalized guidance.

By consistently applying these NLP techniques, you can enhance your self-assurance and develop a more confident mindset. Remember that building confidence is a gradual process, and with practice, you'll experience positive changes in your self-perception and overall well-being.

9. Self Worth

Recognising your self-worth is essential for building a healthy self-esteem and a positive self-image.
 Some steps you can take to recognise and enhance your sense of self-worth:
Practice Self-Reflection: Take time to reflect on your strengths, accomplishments, and positive qualities. Write down your achievements and moments when you felt proud or capable.

Challenge Negative Self-Talk: Become aware of negative thoughts and self-criticism. Challenge these thoughts by asking yourself if they are true, and replace them with affirmations that highlight your worth.

Set Healthy Boundaries: Recognize that you deserve to be treated with respect and kindness. Set boundaries in your relationships and interactions to protect your emotional well-being.

Acknowledge Your Uniqueness: Understand that you are a unique individual with your own set of talents, perspectives, and experiences. Embrace what makes you special.

Celebrate Small Wins: Acknowledge even the smallest achievements and progress you make. Celebrating these victories reinforces your sense of accomplishment.

Practice Self-Compassion: Treat yourself with the same kindness and understanding that you would offer to a friend. Be patient with your mistakes and shortcomings.

Surround Yourself with Positivity: Spend time with people who uplift and support you. Surrounding yourself with positivity can reinforce your sense of self-worth.

Engage in Self-Care: Prioritize self-care activities that nourish your physical, mental, and emotional well-being. Taking care of yourself shows that you value your worth.

Embrace Imperfections: Understand that nobody is perfect, and that imperfections are a natural part of being human. Accepting your flaws helps you recognize your worth despite them.

Set and Achieve Goals: Set realistic goals for yourself and work towards achieving them. Each step forward reinforces your belief in your ability to succeed.

Practice Gratitude: Regularly express gratitude for the positive aspects of your life. Focusing on what you appreciate can boost your self-esteem.

Visualize Your Ideal Self: Imagine the person you want to become, and visualize yourself embodying those qualities. This can inspire confidence and reinforce your sense of worth.

Seek Support: If you struggle to recognize your self-worth, consider seeking guidance from a therapist or counselor. They can help you explore your feelings and develop strategies for building self-esteem.

Remember that recognizing your self-worth is an ongoing process. It involves embracing your strengths, acknowledging your value, and treating yourself with kindness and respect. As you practice these steps, you'll gradually cultivate a stronger sense of self-worth and a healthier self-esteem.

10. Contentment and Fulfilment

Seeking external validation for happiness can lead to dependency on others' opinions, which may not always be consistent or reliable. Cultivating intrinsic happiness is about finding contentment and fulfilment from within.
Here are some ways to shift your focus away from seeking validation and towards finding happiness within yourself:
Self-Awareness: Reflect on why you seek validation from others. Understand the underlying needs and fears that drive this behavior.

Identify Inner Sources of Joy: Explore activities, hobbies, and experiences that genuinely bring you joy and satisfaction. Engaging in these activities can boost your intrinsic happiness.

Set Internal Goals: Focus on personal growth and achievements that are meaningful to you, rather than aiming solely for others' approval.

Practice Self-Compassion: Treat yourself with kindness and understanding, just as you would treat a friend. Forgive yourself for mistakes and embrace your imperfections.

Challenge External Measures: Remind yourself that external validation is temporary and can be unpredictable. Shift your focus to measuring your progress based on your own standards.

Positive Self-Talk: Cultivate a positive inner dialogue. Replace self-doubt and criticism with self-affirming statements that reinforce your self-worth.

Mindfulness: Engage in mindfulness practices to stay present and appreciate the moments as they are, without relying on external factors for happiness.

Celebrate Personal Achievements: Recognize and celebrate your own accomplishments, no matter how small. Your achievements are valid and meaningful.

Embrace Authenticity: Be true to yourself and your values. When you live authentically, you'll naturally attract people who appreciate you for who you are.

Limit Social Media Comparisons: Be mindful of how social media can foster a sense of needing validation. Limit time spent comparing yourself to others online.

Develop Self-Approval: Learn to validate and approve of yourself. Understand that your worth isn't determined by others' opinions.

Practice Gratitude: Focus on the positive aspects of your life and express gratitude for what you have. This shifts your focus from seeking more validation to appreciating what you already possess.

Seek Internal Fulfillment: Find fulfillment in contributing positively to the world around you, whether through acts of kindness, creativity, or helping others.

Set Boundaries: Establish boundaries with those who consistently undermine your self-worth. Surround yourself with people who support and uplift you.

Seek Professional Help: If your quest for external validation significantly affects your well-being, consider seeking guidance from a therapist or counselor to work through these challenges.

Remember, happiness that comes from within is sustainable and empowering. While it's natural to appreciate recognition, your core sense of happiness should be anchored in self-acceptance, self-love, and a genuine sense of fulfillment.

Shifting away from seeking external validation for happiness involves recognizing that your contentment and joy should primarily come from within. Instead of relying on others' opinions to feel fulfilled, focus on understanding your own needs, interests, and aspirations. Engage in activities that genuinely bring you happiness, and set personal goals that resonate with your values. Embrace self-compassion, positive self-talk, and authenticity. Celebrate your accomplishments and practice gratitude for what you have. By prioritizing your own well-being and fostering a strong sense of self-worth, you'll discover a more enduring and meaningful source of happiness that doesn't depend on external validation.

11. Inner Satisfaction

Inner satisfaction serves as a powerful foundation for lasting happiness. It involves finding contentment, fulfillment, and peace within yourself, rather than relying on external factors. Here's a brief explanation of how inner satisfaction contributes to happiness:

Inner satisfaction is the state of being content and fulfilled from within, irrespective of external circumstances or validation. It arises when you align your actions, values, and choices with your authentic self.

By recognizing and appreciating your own worth, accomplishments, and experiences, you cultivate a sense of wholeness and harmony. Inner satisfaction is rooted in self-acceptance, self-love, and mindfulness. It allows you to derive joy from the journey of life itself, appreciating both the highs and lows.

When you prioritize inner satisfaction, you build a resilient source of happiness that isn't dependent on external situations or the opinions of others.

12. Say NO to Competition

Not being competitive entails a shift in mindset and behavior that allows you
Detailed explanation of the benefits and strategies for letting go of excessive competitiveness:
Benefits:
Reduced Stress: Constantly trying to outdo others can create immense pressure and stress. Letting go of competitiveness frees you from this pressure, leading to greater mental and emotional well-being.

Enhanced Self-Esteem: Instead of comparing yourself unfavorably to others, you focus on your own progress. This boosts your self-esteem as you celebrate your achievements without the need for external validation.

Authentic Growth: Without the distraction of competition, you can dedicate your energy to personal growth. You'll develop skills and pursue interests that genuinely resonate with you.

Improved Relationships: Choosing cooperation over competition fosters more genuine and supportive relationships. You'll encourage and uplift others, leading to stronger connections.

Greater Creativity: When you're not constrained by comparison, you're free to explore your creativity and innovative ideas without fear of judgment.

Inner Peace: Letting go of the need to win or prove yourself brings a sense of inner peace. You're no longer driven by the constant pursuit of external validation.

Strategies:

Focus on Personal Goals: Set goals that are meaningful to you, rather than aiming to outdo others. Define success based on your progress and achievements.

Celebrate Others' Success: Instead of feeling threatened by others' accomplishments, genuinely celebrate their successes. This creates a positive and supportive atmosphere.

Practice Self-Compassion: Treat yourself with kindness and understanding, especially when you face challenges or setbacks. Allow yourself to learn and grow without self-criticism.

Collaborate: Seek opportunities to collaborate and share knowledge with others. Working together can lead to better outcomes and shared successes.

Mindfulness: Practice mindfulness to stay present and focused on your own journey. Avoid comparing your progress to others and appreciate the present moment.

Set Boundaries: Avoid engaging in unhealthy competitions or situations that trigger excessive competitiveness. Prioritize your mental well-being.

Embrace Failure: See failure as a chance to learn and improve, rather than a reflection of your worth. This mindset reduces the fear of failure.

Develop Intrinsic Motivation: Cultivate a passion for learning and growth that comes from within. Embrace the joy of the process, not just the end result.

Practice Gratitude: Regularly express gratitude for your own accomplishments and the positive aspects of your life. This shifts your focus away from comparison.

Seek Collaboration: Whenever possible, collaborate with others to achieve shared goals. This helps you contribute positively while letting go of rivalry.

By adopting these strategies, you can gradually shift your mindset away from excessive competitiveness and towards a more fulfilling and harmonious way of living. Remember that this transformation takes time and effort, but the rewards in terms of personal growth and happiness are substantial.

13. Compassion

Cultivating compassion can greatly contribute to your overall happiness and well-being. Compassion involves extending kindness, understanding, and empathy towards yourself and others. Embracing compassion can enhance your happiness:

Self-Acceptance: Compassion allows you to accept yourself, including your flaws and imperfections, without self-judgment. This self-acceptance fosters a positive self-image and boosts your self-esteem.

Reduced Stress: Practicing compassion can help reduce stress by promoting a more relaxed and empathetic outlook. When you're kind to yourself and others, stress and tension decrease.

Positive Relationships: Compassion strengthens your connections with others. It fosters understanding and empathy, which leads to more fulfilling and harmonious relationships.

Emotional Resilience: Compassion enhances your ability to cope with challenges and setbacks. It helps you approach difficulties with a gentler perspective, reducing emotional turmoil.

Increased Joy: When you show compassion towards yourself and others, you contribute to a more positive and joyful atmosphere. Acts of kindness can bring happiness to both the giver and the receiver.

Mindful Awareness: Practicing compassion requires being present and attuned to your emotions and the emotions of others. This mindfulness fosters a deeper sense of connection and understanding.

Enhanced Emotional Intelligence: Compassion contributes to greater emotional intelligence, allowing you to navigate emotions more effectively and respond with empathy.

Generosity and Gratitude: Compassion often leads to acts of generosity, which can bring a sense of fulfillment. It also fosters gratitude as you recognize the positive qualities in yourself and others.

Reduced Isolation: Compassion encourages you to connect with others, reducing feelings of loneliness and isolation. It fosters a sense of belonging and community.

Altruistic Satisfaction: Helping others and showing kindness can lead to a sense of altruistic satisfaction, contributing to your overall sense of well-being.

To embrace compassion for happiness:

Self-Compassion: Treat yourself with kindness and understanding, especially during challenging times. Speak to yourself as you would to a dear friend.

Empathy: Put yourself in others' shoes and try to understand their feelings and perspectives. This fosters deeper connections and compassion.

Practice Acts of Kindness: Engage in small acts of kindness for yourself and others. These acts can be as simple as offering a listening ear or performing a random act of kindness.

Mindful Listening: Practice active and empathetic listening when others share their experiences. This shows that you genuinely care and understand.

Forgiveness: Extend forgiveness to yourself and others. Letting go of resentment and grudges fosters a more compassionate mindset.

Engage in Community: Join groups or initiatives that promote compassion and social support. Contributing to a larger cause can enhance your sense of purpose.

Mindfulness Meditation: Practice mindfulness meditation to cultivate compassion towards yourself and others. This helps develop a compassionate mindset in daily life.

Educate Yourself: Learn about the experiences of others, their challenges, and their triumphs. Understanding diverse perspectives fosters empathy and compassion.

Model Compassion: Lead by example and demonstrate compassion in your interactions with others. Your actions can inspire kindness in those around you.

By incorporating compassion into your daily life, you create a positive ripple effect that not only enhances your own happiness but also contributes to a more compassionate and harmonious world.

14. Awareness

Awareness plays a crucial role in personal growth, self-improvement, and overall well-being. It involves being conscious and present in your thoughts, emotions, actions, and surroundings. Here's how practicing awareness can positively impact your life:

Self-Understanding: Developing self-awareness allows you to understand your thoughts, emotions, strengths, weaknesses, and motivations. This insight empowers you to make informed decisions.

Emotional Regulation: Being aware of your emotions helps you manage them more effectively. You can identify triggers and respond in a balanced and constructive manner.

Mindfulness: Awareness cultivates mindfulness, which involves being fully present in the moment without judgment. This practice reduces stress and increases a sense of calm.

Improved Relationships: When you're aware of your own emotions and reactions, you communicate more authentically and respond empathetically to others. This enhances your interpersonal relationships.

Personal Growth: Recognizing areas for improvement enables you to actively work on self-development. You can set goals, track progress, and evolve as a person.

Stress Reduction: Awareness helps you identify sources of stress and adopt coping strategies. It allows you to manage stressors before they escalate.

Enhanced Decision-Making: With awareness, you can make decisions aligned with your values and goals. You're less likely to be influenced by external pressures.

Effective Communication: Being aware of your own communication patterns and listening attentively to others improves your ability to convey messages clearly and understand others deeply.

Conflict Resolution: Self-awareness helps you recognize your role in conflicts and take responsibility for your actions. This promotes resolution and prevents recurring issues.

Cultivating Gratitude: Being aware of the present moment encourages you to appreciate and find joy in everyday experiences, fostering a sense of gratitude.

To practice awareness:
Mindfulness Meditation: Engage in mindfulness meditation to develop present-moment awareness. Focus on your breath, thoughts, and sensations without judgment.

Journaling: Regularly write down your thoughts, feelings, and experiences. This practice enhances self-reflection and self-awareness.

Check-Ins: Periodically pause during the day to check in with yourself. Notice your emotions, physical sensations, and thoughts.

Body Scan: Consciously scan your body from head to toe, paying attention to any tension, discomfort, or sensations.

Practice Active Listening: When conversing with others, truly listen without thinking about your response. This enhances your understanding and empathy.

Reflect on Actions: At the end of the day, reflect on your actions and interactions. Assess whether they aligned with your values and intentions.

Engage in Mindful Activities: Engage in activities like walking, eating, or even washing dishes with full attention. Notice the sensory experiences involved.

Embrace Solitude: Spend time alone to reflect and connect with your thoughts and feelings without distractions.

Accept Imperfections: Practice self-compassion by accepting your imperfections and mistakes without self-judgment.

Seek Feedback: Invite feedback from trusted individuals to gain external perspectives on your behavior and actions.

By embracing awareness, you develop a deeper connection with yourself, your experiences, and your surroundings. This heightened consciousness fosters personal growth, better relationships, and an overall sense of fulfillment and well-being.

15. Positive Neural Pathways

Teaching your neurons to be happy, icultivate positive neural pathways and habits that contribute to your overall well-being. This process is based on the concept of neuroplasticity, which suggests that your brain can adapt and change throughout your life. Guide your brain towards happiness:

Practice Gratitude: Regularly acknowledge and appreciate the positive aspects of your life. This helps create neural pathways associated with gratitude and positivity.

Positive Self-Talk: Replace negative self-talk with positive affirmations. This rewires your brain to focus on self-compassion and self-encouragement.

Mindfulness Meditation: Engage in mindfulness practices that help you stay present and non-judgmental. These practices strengthen neural connections related to emotional regulation and stress reduction.

Cultivate Positive Habits: Establish routines that align with your well-being, such as exercising, eating nutritious foods, and getting enough sleep. Consistently engaging in these habits reinforces their positive impact on your brain.

Physical Activity: Regular exercise triggers the release of endorphins, the "feel-good" chemicals. This strengthens the connection between physical activity and happiness.

Social Connections: Spend time with loved ones and engage in meaningful social interactions. Positive social experiences contribute to neural pathways associated with happiness and connection.

Practice Acts of Kindness: Engage in acts of kindness for others. These actions activate brain areas related to empathy and compassion.

Engage in Hobbies: Pursue activities that bring you joy and a sense of accomplishment. These experiences help create positive associations and strengthen related neural connections.

Visualization: Imagine positive scenarios and outcomes. This can stimulate brain areas associated with happiness and optimism.

Limit Negative Inputs: Reduce exposure to negative news, content, and influences that might trigger stress or negativity.

Learn and Grow: Continuously challenge your brain by acquiring new knowledge, skills, or hobbies. This promotes cognitive flexibility and creates neural diversity.

Seek Professional Help: If you struggle with persistent negative emotions, consider seeking guidance from a therapist. They can provide strategies tailored to your needs.

Remember that cultivating happiness through neural pathways requires consistent effort and practice. Over time, these positive habits and thought patterns become more natural and contribute to an improved sense of well-being.

Teaching your neurons to be happy involves harnessing the power of neuroplasticity to create positive changes in your brain's structure and function. By consciously engaging in activities that promote happiness, you can shape your brain's neural pathways to lean towards positivity and well-being. Practicing gratitude, positive self-talk, and mindfulness meditation helps forge connections that amplify feelings of contentment and resilience. Engaging in regular physical activity, fostering social connections, and pursuing hobbies you love strengthens neural networks associated with happiness and joy. As you limit exposure to negativity and engage in acts of kindness, your brain responds by reinforcing pathways linked to empathy and compassion. Embracing growth, learning, and seeking professional help when needed also contribute to a brain that is wired for happiness. With consistent effort, you can guide your brain towards a state of greater happiness and emotional well-being.

16. Exercise

Regular exercise has a profound impact on both physical and mental well-being, including the brain's function and happiness. Engaging in physical activity increases blood flow to the brain, which in turn has several positive effects on your mood and cognitive function:

Endorphin Release: Exercise triggers the release of endorphins, neurotransmitters that are often referred to as "feel-good" chemicals. These endorphins interact with receptors in the brain that reduce pain perception and create a sense of euphoria and happiness.

Stress Reduction: Physical activity helps reduce stress by decreasing the production of stress hormones such as cortisol. Elevated stress levels can contribute to feelings of anxiety and unhappiness, while exercise helps alleviate these symptoms.

Improved Mood: Regular exercise has been linked to an improved overall mood and reduced symptoms of depression. It stimulates the release of neurotransmitters like serotonin, which plays a crucial role in regulating mood and emotions.

Enhanced Cognitive Function: Increased blood flow to the brain during exercise can improve cognitive functions such as memory, concentration, and problem-solving skills. This cognitive boost contributes to a greater sense of well-being.

Neuroplasticity: Physical activity supports neuroplasticity, the brain's ability to adapt and change. It promotes the growth of new neurons and strengthens existing connections, which can positively influence happiness and cognitive abilities.

Better Sleep: Regular exercise can improve the quality of your sleep. Adequate sleep is essential for mood regulation and emotional well-being.

Social Interaction: Engaging in group exercises or sports can provide social interactions, which contribute to feelings of connectedness and happiness.

Sense of Achievement: Setting and achieving exercise goals can lead to a sense of accomplishment and self-efficacy, both of which contribute to a positive self-image and happiness.

Mind-Body Connection: Engaging in exercises like yoga and tai chi emphasizes the mind-body connection, fostering relaxation and mental clarity.

Long-Term Benefits: Consistent exercise over time is associated with improved mental resilience and a reduced risk of mental health issues.

Incorporating regular physical activity into your routine can have a profound impact on your overall happiness and well-being. Whether it's a brisk walk, a yoga session, a jog, or any form of exercise you enjoy, the positive effects on your brain's blood flow and neurotransmitter balance can significantly contribute to a happier and healthier life.

17. Happy Hormones

"Happy hormones" refer to the neurotransmitters and chemicals in the brain that play a key role in regulating mood and promoting feelings of happiness and well-being. Here are some of the main "happy hormones" and how they contribute to your emotional state:

Endorphins: These natural painkillers are released during physical activities like exercise, laughter, and certain foods. They create a sense of euphoria and help alleviate stress and pain, contributing to feelings of pleasure and happiness.

Serotonin: Often referred to as the "feel-good" neurotransmitter, serotonin helps regulate mood, appetite, and sleep. Adequate serotonin levels are associated with positive emotions, and low levels can lead to feelings of depression and anxiety.

Dopamine: This neurotransmitter is associated with pleasure, reward, and motivation. It's released when you accomplish goals, experience excitement, or engage in enjoyable activities. Dopamine plays a role in creating positive reinforcement for certain behaviors.

Oxytocin: Often called the "love hormone," oxytocin is released during social bonding, physical touch, and nurturing behaviors. It promotes feelings of trust, empathy, and connection, fostering positive relationships and emotional well-being.

GABA (Gamma-Aminobutyric Acid): GABA is an inhibitory neurotransmitter that helps calm the brain and reduce anxiety. It promotes relaxation and counteracts the effects of stress, contributing to a sense of tranquility and happiness.

Norepinephrine: This hormone and neurotransmitter plays a role in the body's fight-or-flight response to stress. In moderate levels, it can enhance focus, attention, and motivation, contributing to a positive mood.

Endocannabinoids: These naturally occurring compounds are similar to the active compounds in cannabis. They play a role in regulating mood, stress response, and pain perception.

Peptide Hormones: Hormones like ghrelin and leptin, which regulate appetite and energy balance, can indirectly impact mood and emotions. Balanced eating habits can influence the release of these hormones and contribute to emotional well-being.

Promoting the release and balance of these "happy hormones" involves engaging in activities that stimulate their production. Regular exercise, laughter, social interactions, positive experiences, and engaging in hobbies you enjoy can all contribute to a healthier balance of these neurotransmitters. Additionally, practicing mindfulness, managing stress, and maintaining a healthy lifestyle can help support the optimal functioning of these hormones and contribute to your overall happiness.

18. Stress Hormones

While there aren't hormones specifically referred to as "sad hormones," certain neurotransmitters and chemicals in the brain can contribute to feelings of sadness, stress, or negative emotions. Here are some of the key neurotransmitters associated with such emotions:

Cortisol: Although not a hormone, cortisol is a stress hormone released by the adrenal glands in response to stress and perceived threats. Elevated cortisol levels over extended periods can contribute to feelings of anxiety, restlessness, and irritability.

Norepinephrine: While norepinephrine can enhance focus and attention in moderation, excessive levels can contribute to feelings of stress, nervousness, and agitation.

Glutamate: Glutamate is an excitatory neurotransmitter that plays a role in learning and memory. Imbalances in glutamate levels have been linked to conditions like anxiety, depression, and mood disorders.

Cytokines: These proteins are part of the immune system response to inflammation and stress. Chronic inflammation and elevated cytokine levels have been associated with depressive symptoms.

Histamine: Histamine, typically associated with allergic reactions, also plays a role in regulating mood and sleep. Imbalances in histamine levels can contribute to mood disturbances.

Ghrelin: Known as the "hunger hormone," ghrelin stimulates appetite. Fluctuations in ghrelin levels can affect mood and may contribute to emotional eating.

It's important to note that emotions and mood are complex and influenced by a combination of factors, including genetics, environment, life experiences, and brain chemistry. While these neurotransmitters can influence emotions, they are part of a larger interconnected system.

If you're experiencing persistent feelings of sadness, it's advisable to seek support from a mental health professional. They can help assess your situation, provide guidance, and offer appropriate interventions to improve your emotional well-being.

While it's not possible to entirely stop the release of certain neurotransmitters associated with negative emotions, you can take steps to promote the release of "happy hormones" and manage the impact of negative emotions. Here's how you can work towards releasing more "happy hormones" and improving your overall emotional well-being:

Regular Exercise: Engage in regular physical activity, as it promotes the release of endorphins, dopamine, and serotonin—hormones associated with happiness and well-being.

Healthy Eating: Consume a balanced diet rich in nutrients that support brain health. Omega-3 fatty acids, B vitamins, and antioxidants can positively influence neurotransmitter function.

Get Adequate Sleep: Prioritize getting enough sleep, as sleep plays a critical role in regulating mood and maintaining a healthy brain.

Practice Mindfulness and Meditation: Mindfulness practices and meditation can reduce stress, enhance emotional regulation, and promote the release of calming neurotransmitters.

Engage in Activities You Enjoy: Pursue hobbies and activities that bring you joy, as these experiences stimulate the release of dopamine and create positive associations.

Social Interaction: Spend time with friends and loved ones to stimulate the release of oxytocin and promote positive emotions.

Practice Gratitude: Regularly acknowledge the positive aspects of your life to stimulate the release of dopamine and foster a positive outlook.

Laugh and Have Fun: Engage in activities that make you laugh and experience joy, as laughter triggers the release of endorphins.

Engage in Positive Self-Talk: Cultivate a positive internal dialogue to support a healthy mindset and counteract negative emotions.

Limit Stress: Manage stress through relaxation techniques, deep breathing, and effective time management to prevent excessive cortisol release.

Express Creativity: Engage in creative activities like art, music, or writing to stimulate the release of dopamine and enhance mood.

Connect with Nature: Spending time in nature has been shown to positively impact mood and reduce stress.

Seek Professional Help: If you're struggling with persistent negative emotions, consider reaching out to a mental health professional for guidance and support.
Remember that emotions are a natural part of being human, and experiencing a range of emotions is normal. The goal isn't to eliminate negative emotions entirely but to manage them effectively and promote overall well-being by fostering positive experiences and habits

19. Pet & Happy Hormones

Pets can indeed have a positive impact on your emotional well-being and hormonal balance. Interacting with pets, such as dogs, cats, or even other animals like rabbits or birds, has been shown to promote the release of "happy hormones" while also helping to control cortisol levels. Here's how pets can contribute to your overall happiness:

Release of Happy Hormones:

> Oxytocin: Interacting with pets, especially through physical touch like petting or cuddling, can stimulate the release of oxytocin, the "love hormone." Oxytocin fosters feelings of bonding, trust, and connection, promoting a sense of happiness and well-being.
>
> Endorphins: Spending time with pets, engaging in play, and even just watching them can trigger the release of endorphins, which contribute to feelings of joy and pleasure.

Stress Reduction:

> Cortisol Regulation: Studies have shown that spending time with pets can help lower cortisol levels, effectively reducing stress. The calming and soothing presence of a pet can help mitigate the body's stress response.

Enhanced Mood:

> Serotonin and Dopamine: The interaction and companionship provided by pets can lead to increased serotonin and dopamine levels. These neurotransmitters play a crucial role in regulating mood and promoting positive emotions.

Social Connection:
- Reduced Loneliness: Pets provide companionship and reduce feelings of isolation, which can positively impact mental health and happiness.
- Social Interaction: Walking a dog or engaging in pet-related activities can also lead to social interactions with other pet owners, further enhancing your sense of connection.

Routine and Responsibility:
- Structure: Taking care of a pet creates a routine and structure in your life, which can provide a sense of purpose and stability, contributing to overall well-being.

Mindfulness and Mind-Body Connection:
- Presence: Interacting with pets encourages being present in the moment, promoting mindfulness and reducing stress.
- Physical Activity: Activities like playing with pets or taking them for walks encourage physical activity, which has numerous benefits for mental and physical health.

It's important to note that while pets can have many positive effects on emotional well-being, they also come with responsibilities. Owning a pet requires time, effort, and resources, so it's essential to ensure that you can provide proper care and attention. If you're considering getting a pet, make sure to choose one that aligns with your lifestyle and needs.

Ultimately, the companionship and unconditional love that pets provide can significantly contribute to a happier and healthier life, benefiting both your emotional well-being and your physical health.

How pets can help in releasing happy hormones and controlling cortisol:

Oxytocin Release: Spending time with your pet, whether through cuddling, petting, or simply being in their presence, triggers the release of oxytocin. This hormone fosters feelings of bonding, love, and connection, promoting a sense of happiness and well-being.

Endorphin Boost: Interacting with pets, playing with them, or even watching them can lead to the release of endorphins, which are natural mood enhancers. This can lead to feelings of joy, pleasure, and relaxation.

Stress Reduction: The companionship of pets has been shown to lower cortisol levels, reducing stress. Their presence and affection can provide comfort and a sense of calm, helping to manage the body's stress response.

Serotonin and Dopamine Increase: Engaging with your pet, taking them for walks, and enjoying their playful behavior can lead to increased levels of serotonin and dopamine. These neurotransmitters play a crucial role in regulating mood and promoting positive emotions.

Reduced Loneliness: Pets provide companionship, reducing feelings of loneliness and isolation. This social interaction contributes to improved emotional well-being.

Routine and Responsibility: Taking care of a pet establishes a routine, adding structure to your life. The responsibility of caring for them provides a sense of purpose and can positively impact your mental health.

Mindfulness and Presence: Spending time with pets encourages mindfulness, as you focus on the present moment while interacting with them. This can help reduce stress and promote a sense of calm.

Physical Activity: Activities like walking a dog or playing with a pet encourage physical movement. Regular exercise is known to release endorphins and improve mood.

Unconditional Love: Pets offer unconditional love and non-judgmental companionship. This kind of emotional support can greatly contribute to your overall happiness and well-being.

Social Interaction: Owning a pet can lead to social interactions with other pet owners, fostering a sense of community and connection.

It's important to choose a pet that aligns with your lifestyle, needs, and capabilities to ensure a positive experience for both you and the animal. Responsible pet ownership requires commitment and care to provide a loving and supportive environment for your furry friend, ultimately leading to a mutually beneficial relationship that enhances your happiness and reduces stress.

An example of how having a pet can help in releasing happy hormones and controlling cortisol:
Imagine you come home after a long, stressful day at work. As you open the door, your dog excitedly rushes to greet you, wagging its tail and expressing pure joy at your return. You bend down to pet your dog, and as you stroke its fur, you feel a sense of comfort and relaxation wash over you. This simple act triggers the release of oxytocin, often referred to as the "bonding hormone," which

strengthens your connection with your pet and promotes feelings of love and happiness.

Seeing your dog's playful behavior, you decide to engage in a game of fetch. As you toss the ball and watch your dog chase after it with enthusiasm, you can't help but smile. This physical activity not only provides exercise for your pet but also triggers the release of endorphins, the body's natural mood elevators. You notice that your stress from the day seems to melt away, replaced by a sense of joy and contentment.

Later, you take your dog for a walk in the park. The fresh air, the sights and sounds of nature, and the companionship of your furry friend help you feel more present in the moment. As you engage in this mindful activity, your cortisol levels start to decrease. The combination of physical activity, being outdoors, and the positive interaction with your pet contributes to a sense of calm and relaxation.

Back at home, you settle down with your pet by your side. You stroke its fur and feel a sense of companionship and unconditional love. These moments of connection and comfort trigger the release of serotonin and dopamine, neurotransmitters that enhance your mood and create a feeling of well-being.

Overall, your interactions with your pet throughout the evening have led to the release of "happy hormones" such as oxytocin, endorphins, serotonin, and dopamine. These hormonal responses have helped you manage stress, boost your mood, and create a sense of happiness and contentment. Your pet's presence and the positive experiences you shared have played a significant role in promoting your emotional well-being and contributing to a healthier, happier you.

Interacting with a pet can indeed help release stress and promote relaxation

An example of how spending time with a pet can effectively reduce stress:

Picture a day when you've had a particularly demanding schedule, with work deadlines and various responsibilities weighing heavily on your mind. As you return home, feeling tense and mentally exhausted, your cat is waiting by the door. As you enter, it comes over and rubs against your leg, purring softly. You decide to sit down and spend some quality time with your furry companion. You find a quiet corner, sit down, and start petting your cat. Its soothing purrs and warm presence have an immediate calming effect on you. As you stroke its soft fur, you begin to feel a sense of relaxation and comfort. This physical interaction prompts the release of oxytocin, the "love hormone," which helps reduce stress and promote feelings of connection.

You decide to focus your attention solely on your cat's behavior—how it stretches, rolls over, and engages in playful movements. This mindfulness of your pet's actions helps shift your focus away from your stressors and into the present moment. Your breathing becomes slower and more even, and you start to feel a sense of tranquility.

As you continue to interact with your cat, you notice your worries and tension gradually melting away. This experience triggers the release of endorphins, which act as natural pain relievers and mood enhancers. Your cat's presence provides a distraction from your stressors and triggers the relaxation response, reducing the levels of cortisol—the stress hormone—in your body.

As time goes by, you realize that your mood has significantly improved. The stress that you carried from the day has subsided, replaced by a sense of calm and well-being. Your pet's companionship and the moments of connection you shared have effectively helped you release stress, relax, and find a moment of respite from the demands of daily life.

In this way, spending time with your pet can serve as a wonderful way to alleviate stress, foster relaxation, and promote a positive emotional state.

20. Emotional Health & Happiness

Emotional health and happiness are closely intertwined aspects of overall well-being. Emotional health refers to your ability to understand, manage, and express your emotions in a balanced and constructive manner. Happiness, on the other hand, is a positive emotional state characterized by feelings of contentment, joy, and satisfaction.

How emotional health and happiness are interconnected:

Emotional Awareness: Being emotionally healthy involves being aware of your emotions, understanding their origins, and acknowledging their impact on your thoughts and behavior. This self-awareness is crucial for identifying what brings you happiness and addressing any emotional challenges.

Emotional Regulation: Emotional health includes the skill of regulating your emotions effectively. When you can manage negative emotions like stress, anger, and sadness, you create space for positive emotions like happiness to flourish.

Positive Coping: An emotionally healthy individual possesses coping strategies to manage stress and adversity. Developing healthy ways to cope with challenges can prevent prolonged negative emotions that could hinder happiness.

Resilience: Emotional well-being fosters resilience—the ability to bounce back from setbacks. Resilience allows you to navigate difficult situations without losing sight of your overall happiness.

Relationships: Emotionally healthy individuals are better equipped to establish and maintain healthy relationships. Positive connections contribute to happiness, while supportive relationships provide emotional support during tough times.

Gratitude and Positive Perspective: Emotional health nurtures the ability to appreciate the positive aspects of life and maintain a positive perspective. Gratitude and optimism are key components of happiness.

Self-Compassion: Being emotionally healthy involves treating yourself with kindness and self-compassion. This self-care supports happiness by promoting a positive self-image and self-worth.

Mindfulness: Emotionally healthy individuals often practice mindfulness, which involves staying present and non-judgmental. This practice can enhance your ability to savor positive experiences and reduce rumination on negative thoughts.

Personal Growth: Emotional health encourages self-growth and personal development. Engaging in activities that challenge and fulfill you contributes to a sense of accomplishment and happiness.
Expression of Positive Emotions: Emotionally healthy individuals are more likely to express positive emotions openly. Sharing joy, laughter, and love not only enhances personal happiness but also creates positive interactions with others.
It's important to note that emotional health doesn't mean being happy all the time; rather, it's about maintaining a balanced emotional state that allows you to navigate a range of emotions effectively. By cultivating emotional awareness, practicing self-care, and developing healthy coping mechanisms, you can enhance both your emotional well-being and overall happiness.

21. Empathy

Empathy is the ability to understand and share the feelings, perspectives, and experiences of others. It involves stepping into someone else's shoes and trying to grasp their emotions and thoughts without judgment. Empathy is an important aspect of emotional intelligence and plays a significant role in fostering positive relationships, communication, and overall well-being. How empathy contributes to emotional health and happiness: Connection: Empathy enhances your ability to connect with others on a deeper level. When you genuinely understand and acknowledge someone's feelings, it creates a sense of emotional closeness and fosters stronger relationships.

Effective Communication: Empathetic listening and communication involve not only hearing the words but also understanding the emotions behind them. This promotes effective and meaningful interactions, leading to clearer understanding and better relationships.

Reduced Conflict: When you can empathize with others, you're more likely to approach disagreements with understanding and a desire to find common ground. This reduces the potential for misunderstandings and conflicts.

Positive Impact on Mental Health: Practicing empathy can positively impact your mental well-being. It encourages a more compassionate and open-minded outlook, which in turn can contribute to lower levels of stress and anxiety.

Enhanced Emotional Regulation: Empathy helps you recognize and regulate your own emotions more effectively. Understanding the emotions of others helps you better understand and manage your own emotional responses.

Promotion of Altruism: Empathy often leads to acts of kindness and altruism. Helping others and making a positive difference can provide a sense of fulfillment and contribute to your own happiness.

Building Trust: When people feel understood and valued through empathy, it builds trust and rapport. Trust is an essential foundation for healthy relationships, which in turn support emotional well-being.

Cultivation of Compassion: Empathy is closely linked to compassion—the desire to alleviate the suffering of others. Cultivating compassion contributes to a more positive and caring outlook on life.

Enhanced Perspective-Taking: Empathy involves seeing situations from different viewpoints. This broadens your perspective and promotes a more open-minded and flexible attitude, which can lead to greater happiness.

Social Support: Practicing empathy encourages a supportive network of friends, family, and peers. Feeling understood and supported contributes to emotional resilience and overall happiness.

To cultivate empathy:
Active Listening: Pay close attention when others are speaking and show genuine interest in their thoughts and feelings.

Put Yourself in Their Shoes: Try to imagine how the other person feels and what they might be going through.

Validate Emotions: Acknowledge and validate the emotions of others, even if you don't necessarily agree with them.

Ask Open-Ended Questions: Encourage people to share their feelings by asking open-ended questions that invite deeper conversation.

Practice Mindfulness: Be present and fully engaged when interacting with others to better understand their emotions and reactions.

By incorporating empathy into your interactions and relationships, you can enhance your emotional health, promote harmonious connections, and contribute to your overall happiness.

While empathy is a valuable and important trait, excessive empathy can sometimes lead to emotional exhaustion and difficulty in setting boundaries.
Some strategies to help you manage and control too much empathy:
Self-Awareness: Recognize when your empathy is becoming overwhelming. Pay attention to signs of emotional exhaustion or feeling drained after empathetic interactions.

Set Boundaries: Establish clear boundaries to prevent yourself from getting emotionally overwhelmed. It's okay to empathize without taking on someone else's emotional burden entirely.

Practice Self-Care: Prioritize self-care to recharge your emotional energy. Engage in activities that bring you joy and relaxation, and ensure you're taking care of your physical and mental well-being.

Limit Exposure: If certain situations or people consistently trigger excessive empathy, consider limiting your exposure to them or seeking support in managing your emotions.

Develop Empathy Skills: Enhance your ability to differentiate between feeling empathetic and absorbing others' emotions. Practice active listening and understanding without internalizing everything.

Emotional Regulation Techniques: Learn techniques like deep breathing, mindfulness, and meditation to manage your emotional responses and prevent becoming overwhelmed.

Practice Detachment: While staying empathetic, remind yourself that you can support others without fully immersing yourself in their emotions.

Seek Support: Talk to friends, family, or a therapist about your feelings and experiences. Sharing your emotions can help you process and manage them.

Prioritize Your Needs: Remember that taking care of yourself allows you to offer more effective support to others. Make sure your well-being isn't compromised by excessive empathy.

Redirect Focus: Shift your focus towards finding solutions or providing practical support rather than solely absorbing emotional distress.

Practice Saying No: It's okay to decline when you're not emotionally equipped to offer support. Saying no doesn't mean you lack empathy; it means you're taking care of yourself.

Reflect on Impact: Consider whether your excessive empathy is positively or negatively affecting your well-being and the well-being of others. Adjust your approach as needed.

Seek Professional Guidance: If excessive empathy consistently causes distress, consider consulting a therapist who can provide strategies for managing your emotions.

Remember that finding a healthy balance between empathy and self-care is important for your overall well-being. By implementing these strategies, you can control excessive empathy and ensure that your empathetic nature doesn't hinder your emotional health.

Setting boundaries with empathy involves establishing limits on the emotional energy you invest in others while still maintaining a compassionate and caring approach. Here's an example of how you might set boundaries in a situation where you feel your empathy is becoming overwhelming:
Scenario: Supporting a Friend in Need
Imagine you have a friend who often comes to you for emotional support. Lately, they've been going through a difficult time, and you've been spending a lot of time listening to their problems and providing advice. While you genuinely want to help, you've noticed that their emotional struggles are starting to affect your own well-being.
Setting Boundaries:
Self-Assessment: Reflect on your own emotional state and energy levels. Recognize if you're starting to feel emotionally drained or overwhelmed by your friend's issues.

Choose a Communication Approach: Decide how you want to communicate your boundaries to your friend. It can be in person, through a phone call, or even a text message, depending on what feels comfortable for you.

Express Empathy and Concern: Begin by expressing your empathy for your friend's situation. Let them know that you care about their well-being and are here to support them.

State Your Boundaries: Politely and assertively communicate your need for boundaries. For example: "I truly want to be there for you, but I've noticed that I'm starting to feel emotionally overwhelmed by the frequency and intensity of our conversations. I need to set some boundaries to take care of my own well-being."

Be Specific: Clearly state the boundaries you're setting. For instance: "I'm more than happy to continue supporting you, but I need to limit our conversations to a certain time or day so that I can also focus on my own self-care."

Offer Alternatives: Suggest other sources of support, such as recommending professional help or encouraging them to reach out to other friends or family members.

Reiterate Care: Reassure your friend that your decision to set boundaries doesn't diminish your care for them. Emphasize that you're doing this to ensure you can continue to be a supportive friend.

Stay Firm: If your friend tries to push your boundaries, gently remind them of your need for balance. You can say, "I understand that this is important, but I need to stick to the boundaries we've discussed."

Check-In: After a while, check in with your friend to see how they're doing and how they're managing. This demonstrates that you still care while respecting your boundaries.

Setting boundaries in this way allows you to maintain a compassionate approach while safeguarding your emotional well-being. Remember that setting boundaries is a healthy practice that promotes your own self-care and ensures you can continue to offer support in a sustainable manner.

22. Indifference is Unhealthy

Being indifferent to serious events is not typically a healthy or productive response. Indifference implies a lack of concern or interest, which can prevent you from engaging with important matters in a meaningful way. While it's important to manage your emotional responses to prevent becoming overwhelmed, complete indifference can have negative consequences. Here's why:

Lack of Empathy: Indifference can lead to a lack of empathy, making it difficult to connect with the emotions and experiences of others. Empathy helps build connections and understanding, fostering positive relationships and social cohesion.

Missed Opportunities: Being indifferent might cause you to overlook opportunities to learn, grow, and contribute to positive change. Engaging with serious events allows you to stay informed, offer support, and take part in solutions.

Emotional Disconnect: Indifference can lead to emotional detachment, making it challenging to form meaningful connections with people and causes that matter to you. This emotional disconnect can negatively impact your overall well-being.

Social Responsibility: Society benefits when individuals care about important issues and contribute to positive change. Indifference can hinder progress and prevent collective efforts to address challenges.

Impact on Mental Health: While it's important to manage emotional responses, complete indifference might lead to suppression of emotions or avoidance, potentially affecting your mental health over time.

Instead of being indifferent, consider adopting a balanced approach:

Selective Engagement: Choose the issues that resonate with you and align with your values. Focus your attention on causes that you genuinely care about and can contribute positively to.

Mindful Consumption: Stay informed about serious events without becoming overwhelmed. Practice mindful consumption of news and information to prevent emotional overload.

Take Action: If a serious event affects you or aligns with your values, consider taking action. This could involve volunteering, supporting organizations, or participating in discussions that contribute to positive change.

Emotional Regulation: Learn to manage your emotional responses to serious events through techniques like mindfulness, meditation, and self-care. This prevents becoming overwhelmed while staying engaged.

Balance Empathy and Boundaries: Strive for empathetic understanding without taking on excessive emotional burden. Set healthy boundaries to protect your own well-being while still caring.

Stay Open to Learning: Engage with different perspectives and educate yourself about the complexities of serious events. This can lead to personal growth and a more informed perspective.

23. Exercise Engagement

Excessive engagement in tense or stressful situations can indeed lead to unhappiness and negatively impact your well-being. Continuously immersing yourself in stress and tension without proper coping strategies can take a toll on your mental and emotional health. Here's how excessive engrossment in tense situations can contribute to unhappiness:

Chronic Stress: Constant exposure to tense situations can lead to chronic stress, which can disrupt your body's stress response system and negatively affect your mood and overall well-being.

Emotional Exhaustion: Immersing yourself in high-stress situations without taking breaks can lead to emotional exhaustion. Over time, this exhaustion can contribute to feelings of burnout and unhappiness.

Reduced Joy: When you're constantly engrossed in tense situations, you might have less time and mental space for activities that bring you joy and relaxation. This can lead to a lack of balance in your life and decreased overall happiness.

Negative Impact on Relationships: High stress levels can lead to irritability, mood swings, and difficulty managing emotions. This can strain your relationships and make it harder to connect with others, leading to a sense of isolation and unhappiness.

Physical Health Impact: Prolonged stress can have negative effects on your physical health, including weakened immune function, sleep disturbances, and increased risk of various health issues, all of which can contribute to a lower sense of well-being.

To mitigate the impact of excessive engrossment in tense situations on your happiness:

Practice Self-Care: Prioritize self-care activities that help you unwind and relax. Engage in hobbies, exercise, meditation, and other activities that promote relaxation and reduce stress.

Set Boundaries: Establish clear boundaries between work, responsibilities, and personal time. Allow yourself breaks to recharge and disconnect from stressors.

Seek Support: Talk to friends, family, or a mental health professional about your feelings and experiences. Receiving support can help you manage stress and maintain a positive outlook.

Mindfulness and Stress Management: Practice mindfulness techniques and stress management strategies to regulate your emotional responses and prevent becoming overwhelmed.

Time Management: Efficiently manage your tasks and responsibilities to reduce the feeling of being constantly engrossed. Prioritize tasks and allocate time for breaks.

Shift Perspective: Try to view challenges as opportunities for growth and learning rather than as overwhelming stressors. Adopting a positive perspective can help you approach situations with resilience.

Limit Exposure: If possible, limit your exposure to highly tense situations that you have little control over. Focus on areas where you can make a positive impact.

Remember that managing stress and finding balance is essential for maintaining happiness and overall well-being. It's okay to step back, take care of yourself, and seek support when needed to prevent excessive engrossment in tense situations from negatively affecting your happiness.

24. Pursuit To Happiness

The pursuit of happiness and maintaining good health are important goals in life. Striving for happiness and well-being contributes to a fulfilling and meaningful life experience. Here's how prioritising happiness and health can positively impact your overall well-being:

Positive Mindset: Focusing on happiness helps cultivate a positive mindset. A positive outlook can lead to better mental health and improved resilience when facing challenges.

Reduced Stress: Prioritising well-being can help manage stress and prevent its negative effects on your physical and emotional health.

Improved Relationships: When you're happy and healthy, you're better equipped to form positive and meaningful relationships with others.

Enhanced Productivity: Feeling happy and maintaining good health can boost your energy levels and increase your ability to focus and achieve your goals.

Emotional Resilience: Prioritizing happiness helps you build emotional resilience, enabling you to bounce back from setbacks and adapt to changes.

Physical Well-Being: Focusing on health contributes to a stronger immune system, better energy levels, and a decreased risk of various health issues.

Higher Quality of Life: A life characterized by happiness and good health leads to an overall higher quality of life and a greater sense of satisfaction.

Stress Management: Engaging in activities that bring you joy and relaxation can serve as effective stress management techniques.

Positive Habits: Prioritizing health encourages the adoption of healthy habits like regular exercise, balanced nutrition, and adequate sleep.

Longevity: Both happiness and health are linked to a longer life expectancy and a higher likelihood of aging well.

Remember that happiness and health are ongoing pursuits that involve a combination of actions and attitudes. It's essential to find a balance that works for you and prioritize self-care, positivity, and overall well-being.

25. Higher Quality of Life

"Higher quality of life" refers to a state of well-being and contentment that goes beyond mere material wealth or physical comfort. It encompasses various factors that contribute to an individual's overall satisfaction, happiness, and fulfillment in life. A higher quality of life is characterized by a positive and holistic experience that includes both physical and emotional well-being, social connections, personal growth, and a sense of purpose. Here are some key aspects that contribute to a higher quality of life: Physical Health: Good physical health, including proper nutrition, regular exercise, and adequate sleep, plays a significant role in improving the overall quality of life. Feeling physically well can enhance energy levels, reduce the risk of illnesses, and contribute to a greater sense of vitality.

Mental and Emotional Well-Being: Positive mental health, emotional resilience, and the ability to manage stress and challenges effectively contribute to a higher quality of life. A positive mindset and emotional balance lead to greater life satisfaction.

Social Connections: Building and maintaining meaningful relationships with family, friends, and a supportive community enriches life and provides emotional support. Strong social connections are essential for a fulfilling life.

Personal Growth and Development: Engaging in continuous learning, pursuing personal interests, and setting and achieving goals contribute to a sense of accomplishment and personal growth, enhancing overall life satisfaction.

Work-Life Balance: Balancing work and personal life allows for time to relax, enjoy hobbies, spend time with loved ones, and pursue leisure activities that bring joy and relaxation.

Financial Security: While not the sole determinant of quality of life, having financial stability can provide a sense of security and freedom to enjoy life without excessive financial stress.

Environmental Factors: Living in a safe, clean, and supportive environment contributes to a higher quality of life. Access to green spaces, cultural opportunities, and a sense of community can enhance overall well-being.

Cultural and Recreational Activities: Engaging in cultural, creative, and recreational activities that align with personal interests and passions can bring joy and a sense of fulfillment.

Sense of Purpose: Having a sense of purpose or meaning in life, whether through meaningful work, contributions to society, or personal values, contributes to a sense of fulfillment and well-being.

Personal Values and Beliefs: Aligning your life with your values and beliefs fosters authenticity and a sense of inner harmony. Overall, a higher quality of life is a multidimensional concept that encompasses various facets of well-being. It's about experiencing joy, contentment, and a sense of fulfillment across different areas of life. Each individual's definition of a higher quality of life may vary, but it generally involves finding a balance among these different aspects to create a meaningful and satisfying life.

26. Shifting Perspective

Shifting your perspective involves looking at a situation from a different angle or adopting a more positive and constructive viewpoint.

An example of how you might shift your perspective in a challenging situation:

Initial Perspective: You've been facing setbacks in your career and haven't been able to land the job you've been striving for. You're feeling frustrated and discouraged, thinking that your efforts are in vain and that you'll never achieve your career goals.

Shifted Perspective: Instead of dwelling on the setbacks, you decide to shift your perspective and focus on the positive aspects of the situation. You remind yourself that setbacks are a natural part of any journey, and they provide opportunities for growth and learning. You think about the skills and experiences you've gained during your job search, realizing that they have added value to your professional profile. You also consider that sometimes the path to success is not linear, and each challenge is a stepping stone toward your goals. By shifting your perspective, you're able to maintain a positive outlook, see setbacks as valuable learning experiences, and remain motivated to continue working towards your career aspirations.

A few more examples of shifting perspectives in different situations:

Relationship Challenges:

Initial Perspective: A close friend has been distant lately, and you feel hurt and think they might not care about your friendship anymore.

Shifted Perspective: Instead of jumping to conclusions, you consider that your friend might be going through a tough time and could use your support. You decide to reach out and offer a listening ear, understanding that people have their own struggles that can affect their behavior.

Traffic Jam:
Initial Perspective: Stuck in a traffic jam, you're frustrated and irritated that you're wasting valuable time.
Shifted Perspective: Instead of focusing on the delay, you use the extra time to listen to an interesting podcast or enjoy your favorite music. You remind yourself that a slower pace can sometimes offer a chance to unwind and enjoy the journey.

Workload at School/Work:
Initial Perspective: You're overwhelmed by a heavy workload and feel stressed about meeting deadlines.
Shifted Perspective: You remind yourself that challenges at work or school indicate growth and progress. You break down tasks into manageable steps, celebrating small accomplishments along the way, and viewing the workload as an opportunity to develop your skills.

Health and Fitness Journey:
Initial Perspective: After missing a workout session, you feel guilty and consider giving up on your fitness goals.
Shifted Perspective: Instead of dwelling on the missed session, you focus on your consistency overall. You recognize that setbacks are normal and part of the journey, and you're committed to getting back on track with your next workout.

Change in Plans:
Initial Perspective: Your vacation plans get canceled due to unforeseen circumstances, and you're disappointed.
Shifted Perspective: While disappointed, you look for alternative ways to enjoy your time off, such as planning a staycation, exploring local attractions, or using the time for self-care and

relaxation.

Difficult Feedback at Work:
Initial Perspective: You receive constructive criticism at work and feel demotivated, thinking you're not performing well.
Shifted Perspective: Instead of taking it as a negative evaluation, you see the feedback as an opportunity for growth. You appreciate your supervisor's input and plan to work on the areas highlighted for improvement.

Shifting perspectives involves reframing situations to find the silver lining, recognize opportunities for growth, and maintain a positive outlook. It's a valuable skill that can help you navigate challenges with resilience and optimism.

27. Relationships

Managing relationships for happiness involves fostering positive connections, effective communication, and mutual support. Some strategies to help you nurture relationships in a way that contributes to your overall happiness:

Open Communication: Practice honest and open communication with your loved ones. Express your thoughts, feelings, and needs clearly, and encourage them to do the same. Effective communication helps prevent misunderstandings and builds trust.

Active Listening: Pay attention when others are speaking and make an effort to understand their perspective. Avoid interrupting and validate their emotions to show that you value their thoughts.

Quality Time: Spend quality time together engaging in activities you both enjoy. Whether it's a hobby, shared interests, or simply meaningful conversations, investing time in relationships strengthens bonds.

Boundaries: Establish healthy boundaries to ensure both parties feel respected and comfortable. Respect each other's personal space and recognize the importance of individual needs.

Empathy: Put yourself in the other person's shoes and try to understand their feelings and viewpoints. Empathy enhances connection and fosters understanding.

Support and Encouragement: Be a source of support and encouragement for your loved ones. Celebrate their successes, offer a listening ear during challenging times, and provide constructive feedback when needed.

Respect Differences: Embrace and respect each other's differences, whether they're related to opinions, beliefs, or lifestyles. Diversity can enrich relationships and provide opportunities for learning.

Conflict Resolution: Handle conflicts in a constructive manner. Focus on the issue at hand rather than attacking the person. Use "I" statements to express your feelings and work together to find solutions.

Express Gratitude: Show appreciation for the people in your life. Expressing gratitude and acknowledging their contributions can strengthen bonds and create a positive atmosphere.

Apologize and Forgive: Be willing to apologize when you make mistakes and forgive others when they do. Holding onto grudges can hinder the growth and happiness of relationships.

Quality Over Quantity: It's not about the quantity of relationships but the quality. Focus on maintaining a few meaningful connections rather than spreading yourself too thin.

Celebrate Milestones: Mark important occasions and milestones in your loved ones' lives. Whether it's birthdays, achievements, or anniversaries, celebrating together can create lasting memories.

Give Space: Recognize the importance of personal space and alone time. Balancing time spent together with individual pursuits can contribute to a healthier relationship.

Share Responsibilities: In romantic relationships, friendships, and family dynamics, sharing responsibilities and making collaborative decisions can strengthen your sense of teamwork.

Self-Care: Remember to take care of your own well-being. When you're happy and fulfilled individually, you bring positivity and vitality to your relationships.

By cultivating these practices, you can create and maintain relationships that contribute to your happiness, emotional well-being, and sense of connectedness with others.

28. The Truth

An Important Truth is Happiness, Wealth, and Health are all deeply influenced by your internal mindset, attitudes, and choices, rather than solely by external circumstances.
Here's a breakdown of how each of these aspects can be influenced by your internal perspective:
Happiness: Your happiness is largely shaped by your thoughts, attitudes, and perceptions. While external events can impact your emotions temporarily, your overall happiness is determined by how you interpret and respond to those events. Cultivating a positive mindset, practicing gratitude, focusing on meaningful experiences, and nurturing healthy relationships are all internal factors that contribute to your overall happiness.

Wealth: While external factors like financial opportunities and economic conditions play a role in wealth accumulation, your financial well-being is also influenced by your financial habits, mindset, and decisions. Making informed financial choices, practicing budgeting and saving, and pursuing opportunities with determination can significantly impact your financial success.

Health: Physical health is influenced by factors such as genetics and environmental conditions, but your lifestyle choices, habits, and attitudes also play a major role. Regular exercise, balanced nutrition, proper sleep, stress management, and positive self-care practices are all within your control and contribute to your overall health and well-being.

In essence, your internal mindset and choices are powerful determinants of your overall life satisfaction and well-being. While external circumstances can have an impact, you have the ability to shape your own happiness, wealth, and health through your thoughts, behaviors, and actions. By focusing on cultivating a positive mindset, making informed decisions, and adopting healthy habits, you can significantly enhance your quality of life and achieve a greater sense of fulfillment and contentment.

People often look outside themselves for happiness, wealth, and validation due to a combination of societal influences, cultural norms, and personal conditioning. Here are some reasons why individuals may tend to seek these things externally:
Social Comparisons: Society often promotes the idea of success, happiness, and self-worth being linked to external markers such as wealth, possessions, and appearances. This leads people to compare themselves to others and seek validation from external sources.

Cultural Conditioning: Cultural values and beliefs can emphasize the pursuit of external achievements as a measure of success and happiness. These values can influence individuals to prioritize material gains.

Media and Advertising: Media, advertising, and social media often portray images of success and happiness tied to external factors like luxury items, status symbols, and idealized lifestyles, shaping people's desires and expectations.

Immediate Gratification: External sources of pleasure or validation can provide quick and easily accessible gratification, leading individuals to seek happiness in immediate pleasures rather than internal fulfillment.

Fear of Missing Out (FOMO): The fear of missing out on experiences or possessions that others have can drive individuals to seek external achievements in order to feel on par with their peers.

Social Validation: People seek external validation to feel accepted and valued by others. Likes, comments, and approval from others on social media platforms, for instance, can provide a temporary sense of validation.

Lack of Self-Awareness: Many individuals may not be fully aware of the power they have to shape their internal experiences. They may not have learned effective strategies for cultivating happiness and well-being from within.

Despite these external influences, it's important to recognize that true and lasting happiness, wealth, and fulfillment often arise from within. While external factors can provide temporary satisfaction, genuine well-being comes from understanding oneself, embracing one's values, cultivating positive habits, and finding joy in life's experiences. Shifting focus inward and building a strong foundation of internal well-being can lead to a more balanced and fulfilled life.

29. Rewiring

Rewiring your perspective to turn inward involves shifting your focus from external sources of happiness and validation to cultivating a sense of fulfillment, contentment, and self-awareness from within.

The steps you can take to rewire your mindset and prioritize your internal well-being:

Practice Mindfulness: Mindfulness involves being fully present in the moment and observing your thoughts and feelings without judgment. Regular mindfulness meditation can help you become more attuned to your inner experiences and reduce the influence of external distractions.

Self-Reflection: Set aside time for introspection and self-reflection. Journaling about your thoughts, feelings, and goals can help you gain insight into your desires and values.

Identify Core Values: Clarify your core values and beliefs. Understanding what truly matters to you can guide your decisions and actions, helping you align your life with your internal compass.

Challenge Social Comparisons: Recognize the pitfalls of constantly comparing yourself to others. Focus on your own journey, progress, and growth rather than external benchmarks.

Cultivate Gratitude: Regularly acknowledge and appreciate the positive aspects of your life. Gratitude fosters a sense of abundance and contentment.

Practice Self-Compassion: Treat yourself with the same kindness and understanding that you would offer to a friend. Self-compassion reduces self-criticism and nurtures a positive self-image.

Set Intrinsic Goals: Shift your focus from external achievements (extrinsic goals) to personal growth and well-being (intrinsic goals). Pursue activities that bring you joy and fulfillment for their own sake.

Embrace Imperfection: Accept that perfection is unattainable, and that making mistakes is a natural part of growth. Embracing imperfection allows you to approach challenges with resilience and a positive attitude.

Practice Self-Care: Prioritize self-care activities that nourish your mind, body, and soul. Engaging in activities you love boosts your overall well-being.

Limit External Validation: Reduce your reliance on external validation, such as social media likes and comments. Validate yourself based on your own values and accomplishments.

Develop Resilience: Cultivate resilience by facing challenges with a growth mindset. View setbacks as opportunities for learning and personal development.

Surround Yourself with Positivity: Surround yourself with people who support your journey towards internal well-being and encourage your personal growth.

Disconnect from Distractions: Take breaks from constant external stimuli, such as technology and media, to give yourself space for introspection.

Learn from Experience: Reflect on past experiences and lessons. Use your experiences as opportunities for growth and insight.

Seek Professional Guidance: If you find it challenging to shift your perspective, consider seeking support from a therapist or counselor who can provide guidance on cultivating an inward-focused mindset.

Rewiring your mindset to turn inside takes time and consistent effort. It involves a journey of self-discovery and personal growth, ultimately leading to a deeper sense of contentment, fulfillment, and a more authentic life aligned with your internal values and desires.

30. DREAM, ASK, BELIEVE, RECEIVE, REPEAT :
The Cycle of Manifestation"

"Dream, Ask, Believe, Receive, Repeat" forms a powerful framework that bridges the gap between imagination and reality, fostering a journey of manifestation and transformation.

Dream: At the core of this process lies the act of dreaming. Your dreams are the canvas upon which you paint your aspirations, envisioning a life filled with possibilities. Dreams are the fuel that ignites the journey towards your goals.

Ask: With clarity and intention, you articulate your desires and set precise goals. You ask the universe or your inner self for what you truly want. This step involves defining your ambitions, creating a roadmap towards your vision.

Believe: Belief acts as the anchor in this journey. It's the unwavering faith that your dreams are attainable. Cultivating a positive and unwavering mindset allows you to overcome doubts and obstacles, and it infuses your actions with the conviction that success is possible.

Receive: As you hold steadfast to your dreams and beliefs, you open yourself to the energy of receiving. Opportunities, synchronicities, and resources align themselves with your intentions. Being receptive allows you to recognize and embrace the pathways that lead to your desires.

Repeat: The journey of manifestation is not a one-time event; it's a cycle of perpetual renewal. Repeating this process ensures that you remain aligned with your goals, reinforcing your intentions, and maintaining the positive energy needed for manifestation.

"Dream, Ask, Believe, Receive, Repeat" serves as a reminder that the power to shape your reality lies within you. By infusing each step with intention, positivity, and action, you orchestrate a symphony of transformation that turns dreams into tangible achievements.

While the "Dream ask, believe, receive, repeat" concept can be motivating and encouraging, it's important to recognize that achieving goals and desires typically involves a combination of factors, including effort, planning, adaptability, and external circumstances. The process described in this phrase aligns with the idea that focusing on positive thoughts and intentions can influence your actions and choices, ultimately shaping your outcomes. However, it's also important to temper this approach with a realistic understanding of life's complexities and challenges. Manifestation involves both internal and external factors, and while positive thinking can play a role, taking proactive steps and staying adaptable are also essential for achieving your goals.

31. Brain Training

Training the brain to lead a fulfilling life involves cultivating positive habits, optimizing cognitive function, and fostering a mindset that supports well-being.

How to work on training your brain for a fulfilling life:

Mindfulness and Meditation: Regular mindfulness and meditation practices can help you cultivate self-awareness, reduce stress, and enhance your emotional regulation. These practices can promote a sense of peace and well-being.

Positive Affirmations: Use positive affirmations to rewire your brain for optimism and self-confidence. Repeatedly affirming positive statements about yourself can influence your self-perception and boost your overall mindset.

Gratitude Practice: Cultivate gratitude by reflecting on the things you're thankful for. Gratitude rewires your brain to focus on the positive aspects of life and enhances your overall well-being.

Visualization: Practice visualizing your goals and desired outcomes. Visualization can create a positive mindset and motivate you to take action towards your aspirations.

Healthy Lifestyle: Prioritize physical health through regular exercise, balanced nutrition, and sufficient sleep. Physical well-being has a direct impact on cognitive function and mental health.

Continuous Learning: Engage in lifelong learning to keep your brain active and adaptable. Learning new skills, reading, and pursuing hobbies stimulate brain function and promote cognitive health.

Social Connections: Cultivate meaningful relationships. Positive social interactions contribute to brain health and emotional well-being.

Practice Resilience: Develop resilience by embracing challenges and setbacks as opportunities for growth. Resilience helps you navigate life's ups and downs with a positive attitude.

Limit Negative Influences: Reduce exposure to negative news, toxic relationships, and stressors that can impact your mental state.

Practice Kindness: Acts of kindness and helping others can trigger positive emotions and create a sense of fulfillment.

Set and Pursue Goals: Setting and working towards meaningful goals provides a sense of purpose and achievement. Celebrate your progress along the way.

Positive Self-Talk: Challenge and reframe negative self-talk. Replace self-criticism with self-compassion and encouragement.

Limit Multitasking: Focus on one task at a time to enhance productivity and cognitive function.

Embrace Creativity: Engage in creative activities that stimulate your imagination and contribute to a sense of fulfillment.

Mind-Body Connection: Recognize the connection between your mental and physical well-being. Practices like yoga and deep breathing exercises can promote relaxation and holistic health.

While these practices are not "supernatural," they are rooted in neuroscience, psychology, and personal development. By actively working on training your brain and adopting positive habits, you can create a fulfilling and enriched life experience. Remember that change takes time and consistency, so be patient with yourself as you cultivate these habits and reshape your mindset.

"Incorporating **GRATITUDE** into our daily lives is a powerful tool that can lead to lasting health and happiness. It involves taking a step back to acknowledge the positive aspects of our existence, no matter how small they may seem.

By focusing on what we're thankful for, we redirect our attention away from stress and negativity.

This simple practice has a ripple effect on our well-being. It can enhance our mental and emotional health, boost our resilience during challenging times, and even improve our physical health by reducing stress-related ailments.

Throughout this journey, we'll delve into various gratitude exercises and techniques that you can easily integrate into your routine, helping you harness the transformative power of gratitude for a happier and healthier life."

In the realm of health and happiness, the principles of Neuro-Linguistic Programming (NLP) offer a valuable toolkit for personal transformation and holistic well-being. NLP empowers individuals to reshape their mindset, communication patterns, and behaviors to achieve a balanced and fulfilling life. By recognizing the interplay between thoughts, language, and actions, individuals can harness the power of their own minds to promote mental and physical health while nurturing happiness.
Through NLP techniques, individuals can navigate challenges with resilience, manage stress through effective communication with themselves and others, and break free from negative thought patterns that hinder growth. Moreover, NLP promotes self-awareness, enabling individuals to connect with their inner selves and align their aspirations with their values. By reprogramming the

mind with positive affirmations, visualizations, and mindfulness, one can create a solid foundation for happiness and well-being. It's important to remember that NLP is not a supernatural remedy, but a practical and psychological approach grounded in science. The transformation it offers arises from a deep understanding of human psychology, language, and behavior. As individuals integrate NLP principles into their lives, they can experience a profound shift towards healthier habits, meaningful connections, and a more fulfilled existence.

Ultimately, NLP empowers individuals to take charge of their own narrative, unlocking the potential for health and happiness from within. By cultivating a positive mindset, fostering effective communication, and embracing personal growth, NLP becomes a guiding force on the journey towards a life of vitality, positivity, and well-being.

The Miracle Books

The Miracle Books

About the Author

Abha Bhardwaj Sharma, an accomplished professor of English, is the visionary behind **Miracle English Language & Literature Institute,** a journey that commenced in 1998 and has thrived for 25 impactful years. With a holistic approach, she has cultivated a space for nurturing both the intellect and the spirit. Prof. Sharma is not only an educator but also an avid author, penning several noteworthy books including the thought-provoking '**I am a Miracle'** and the extensive four-volume series **"History of English Literature." & other many other books on Literature** Prof. Abha Bhardwaj Sharma's trilogy is a transformative journey through three essential aspects of human life, all viewed through the empowering lens of '**Neuro-Linguistic Programming (NLP)'.** In the first volume, **"Health & Happiness,"** she unravels the secrets to holistic well-being and the pursuit of joy, utilising NLP techniques to guide readers towards a healthier, happier life. The second volume, '**Wealth'** explores the intricacies of financial empowerment and abundance, leveraging NLP principles to reshape readers' mindsets towards wealth creation. Finally, the third volume, '**Love, Romance & Relationships'** delves into the dynamics that shape our connections with others, offering NLP-based insights for nurturing fulfilling and harmonious relationships.

As an educator, writer, visionary, and skilled wordsmith, Prof. Abha Sharma embodies the essence of fostering a love for language and literature, all while nurturing generations of adept scholars. Her legacy is indelibly etched in the hearts and minds of those she has touched, and her influence continues to shape the trajectory of English Language and Literature Education.

Printed in Dunstable, United Kingdom